A Catholic Prays Scripture
(Volume 3)

concerning some biblical characters

Robert Charles Burdett

Unless otherwise noted, scripture texts in this work were taken from the New American Bible, Catholic Parish Edition (1994-1995), copyright, 1970, by Catholic Bible Publishers, Wichita, Kansas 67201.

Notes:
1. Unless otherwise noted, any verse text **emboldened** or removed (as indicated by "…") were made by the author of this book.
2. Clarifications and/or additions by the author are identified by [brackets].
3. In most instances, the quoted verses reflect the original NAB punctuation; but in some cases (for clarity) punctuation marks (typically quote marks) may have been changed or removed.
4. Scripture quotes within the *Catechism of the Catholic Church* paragraphs cited (see below) and/or other quotes identified by endnotes may reflect other Bible translations (as noted in the source documents).

Unless otherwise noted, all "*Catechism*" texts in this work were taken from the English translation of the *Catechism of the Catholic Church* for the United States of America, copyright, 1994 United States Catholic Conference, Inc., as published by Ignatius Press, 2515 McAllister Street, San Francisco, CA 94118.

Notes:
1. The author uses CCC throughout this work to denote quotes from the *Catechism of the Catholic Church*.
2. Unless otherwise noted, any texts **emboldened** or removed (as indicated by "...") were made by the author of this book.
3. Spaced periods (". .") identify text that had been removed in the original CCC text (versus the author of this book, as noted above).

As noted in the "Endnotes and Amplifications" section of this book, the author read and reviewed a variety of publications while writing this book. The author highly recommends all the publications noted to the readers of this book – in order that they more fully understand God, humankind, and his universe.

CONTENTS

Ignorance of the Scriptures is ignorance of Christ.

A Catholic Prays Scripture (Volume 3)
concerning some biblical characters

Introduction

This is the third book in the four-volume series *A Catholic Prays Scripture….* The first book in the series was titled *A Catholic Prays Scripture: and tips for how you can too.* In Chapters 2 (…Prays…) and 4 (Prayer Writing Techniques) of that book, I provided some information that hopefully helped you "pray Scripture." For your convenience, I have condensed those two chapters and included the abridged text in the appendix that you will find at the end of this book.

Note: The other two volumes in this series are titled: A Catholic Prays Scripture (Volume 2): concerning the sacraments; and *A Catholic Prays Scripture (Volume 4): concerning God's "word" and the "future."*

When I got around to organizing all the prayers that I wrote, I noted that a lot of them concerned what I irreverently referred to as "biblical biggies" – the "stars" of the Bible – the ones that have even been portrayed in the movies. I finally settled on the more generic and reverent descriptor of "characters" to categorize the people that found their way into my prayers and into this book.

This book "prays Scripture" concerning biblical characters; and (like most books) there are some main characters (e.g., Abraham, Moses, Mary the Mother of God, St. Paul) and there are some minor characters (e.g., Melchizedek, Uzzah). In this book we will view some characters "up close and personal." Others will just be mentioned in passing. In either case, note the roles that these characters played in salvation history – our salvation history. Note also the theology associated with some of the characters (e.g., the faith of Abraham).

So how many characters are there in the Bible. One source places the number at 3,237. That source notes that there are only 1,794 unique names in the Bible (e.g., there are 31 different Zechariahs).[1] I don't know any of the details behind these numbers. I don't know if they include the deuterocanonical books found in Catholic Bibles. I don't know how the source treated name changes: as Abram became Abraham, Saul became Paul, and Simon became Peter. Let it suffice to say that there are a lot of "characters" in the bible, and I will touch upon only a few in this book – but they for the most part will be "biblical biggies."

By our nature, we humans are interested in other humans – more so than we are interested in ideas or doctrines. As such, much of what we eventually learn about ideas and doctrines comes from our observations of people. That is the scary part about reading magazines like *Us Weekly* and *People* – that is how many of us learn about today's ideas and doctrines.

Four Biblical Images of the Church

"The great Swiss theologian Hans Urs von Balthasar has suggested that four biblical images of the Church, based on four great New Testament figures, shape and reshape the Church in every age.

- The Church of office and jurisdiction is formed in the image of **Peter**, to whom the Lord consigned the keys of the Kingdom.

- The Church of evangelization is formed in the image of **Paul**, apostle to the gentiles.

- The Church of discipleship, formed in the image of **Mary**, whose 'be it done unto me according to your word' was, in a sense, the very beginning of Christian discipleship.

- The Church of contemplative prayer is formed in the image of the apostle **John**, who rested his head on the Lord's breast at the Last Supper."[2]

Question: If you were the pope, how would you order the above biblical images; to what extent would you emphasize these images in the Church today?

My Answer: I have reordered the images above (from the order in the source noted) to reflect my answer to the above question. In my opinion, the most important passage in the Bible (regarding the Church) is Mt 16:17-19.

> *Jesus said to him in reply, "Blessed are you, **Simon** son of Jonah. For flesh and blood has not revealed this to you, but my heavenly Father. And so I say to you, you are **Peter**, and upon this rock I will build my church, and the gates of the netherworld shall not prevail against it. I will give you the keys to the kingdom of heaven. Whatever you bind on earth shall be bound in heaven; and whatever you loose on earth shall be loosed in heaven."*

Your Answer: You might want to reorder the above biblical images to suit your idea of Church. Indeed, that is one of the beauties of the Church – the ability to incorporate a wide range of biblical images – as we collectively try to understand and live the gospel.

You don't have to answer the question now. This book contains chapters on three of the principle images: St. Peter, St. Paul, and Mary the Mother of God.

In this book, I don't write about the last image noted by Hans Urs von Balthasar, the image of the apostle John. If you have access to the first book in this series reread the chapter titled *A Prayer for Revelation*. That chapter contains a lot of information on John, the author of Revelation – the man that I affectionately referred to as "Father John."

Likewise, in the second volume of this series, in the chapter titled *A Prayer for the Fishermen*, there are some additional details on St. Peter, which you may wish to reread before you answer the question posed on the previous page.

The Organization of this Book

There is some logic to the order of the chapters. They progress (more or less) chronologically from the Old Testament characters like Abram/Abraham (first mentioned in Genesis 11:26) to the most prolific New Testament author, St. Paul (first mentioned in Acts 7:58, as "a young man named Saul").

If I were to criticize this book, I would probably complain that there are too many prayers and chapters on those Old Testament "Jewish" characters and not enough prayers and chapters on the New Testament "Christian" characters. This criticism is probably fair, although we Christians certainly have not abandoned the Old Testament.

The table on the following page will give you a feel for the "biblical biggies" that I prayed about as I "prayed Scripture." It will also list some of the minor characters that I will note and some of the subjects/theology that I will address along the way. Hopefully, the table will serve as something of an index (since this book doesn't have one).

You will note in the following table that there will be a lot of information in this book about history and a special subset of history called "sacred history." Some of the books in the Bible that I will write about are historical in nature – the history of the exodus, the history of Israel's battles over the centuries, the details of Jesus' birth, and the early history of the Church that Jesus established on Earth. I will compare history and sacred history, while reminding you that the Bible is a theological book, not a history book. The Bible was written to tell us about God.

The characters that I will write about were important as they relate to "sacred history" – were important as they relate to God. Some had a major impact on sacred history – they were truly "biblical biggies." Others had smaller roles to play. They were the equivalent to the "bit players" that go almost unnoticed in the movies that we watch. But they too had a role to play in salvation history – as do you and me.

Characters, Subjects, and Theology (by chapter)

	Prayer	Star(s)	Others	Subjects and Theology
	Introduction	King Saul King David	An Amalekite youth	History
1	"Abraham's Faith" Prayer	Abram / Abraham	Sarai / Sarah Melchizedek	Faith and Works
2	An "Exodus" Prayer	Moses	Pharaoh Aaron	Free Will Hardheartedness Mercy (Hesed)
3	"The Ark" Prayer	Mary – a Type of Ark Mary – full of grace	Uzzah	Four Senses of Scripture Typology
4	A Tribute to Joshua	Joshua	Moses	Sacred History Memories and Miracles Warriors
5	Daniel's "Dream" Prayer	Daniel	Nebuchadnezzar	Dreams Hellenism
6	A Nativity Prayer	Mary – a Type of Ark Mary – full of grace	Joseph Magi Shepherds	Synoptic Gospels The Infancy Narratives Maryology Marian Doctrines
7	A Prayer of Thanks – for St. Paul	Saul / St. Paul	Simon / Kephas (St. Peter)	St. Paul's gospel St. Paul vs. St. Peter

A Newspaper Account of King Saul's Death

There are a lot of ways to study the "characters" in the Bible. One of the exercises in my Bible study suggested that I imagine myself as a newspaper reporter assigned to write an article on King Saul's death. The article that I wrote is printed on the following page.

If you want to get a feel for the biblical account before proceeding, read the last two chapters from 1 Samuel and the first chapter of 2 Samuel.[3]

As previously noted, I am going to address "history" as it relates to "sacred history" in this book. The newspaper reporter assignment helped me start to think about the relationship between how we view history and facts today; and how we view the sacred history presented in the Bible and the theological facts therein.

Hopefully, the newspaper article on the next page will serve as a little teaser for the information that will follow. Have a little fun with the article. Fact check the article for me. **Did King Saul really try to "nail" King David?**

Man Executed Who Boasted He Slew King

(Ziklag)   An escapee from an Israelite camp boasted to authorities today that he had finished off an injured King Saul. The unidentified Amalekite youth confessed his role in King Saul's death to David today in this dusty and now heavily fire damaged Negeb town, twelve miles northwest of Beer-sheba.

Ziklag, the Philistine town given to David by Achish, the king of Gath, is where David, his men, and their families now reside; although most of the city was recently burned to the ground by raiders from Amalek. David and his six hundred men recently returned to Ziklag, with their recaptured wives and recovered booty, after defeating the Amalekite raiders that had looted the town and set it on fire.

The youthful murderer reported to David that he had, by chance, found himself on Mount Gilboa as King Saul and his troops bravely battled a superior Philistine army. It was at that time that the youth said he saw Saul leaning on his spear, with chariots and horsemen closing in on him. The Amalekite youth reported that Saul then pleaded with him, "Stand up to me, please, and finish me off, for I am in great suffering, yet fully alive." It was at this time that the unidentified youth reported that he "stood up to him (Saul) and dispatched him, for I knew that he could not survive his wound." The youth further reported that he removed Saul's crown and armlet at that time. He indicated during questioning that he had brought both the crown and the armlet to David.

The Amalekite youth also reported that many of Saul's troops had fallen during the battle on Mount Gilboa and that Saul's son, Jonathan, had also perished in the heavy fighting that had taken place during the battle with the Philistines.

More stories from the battlefield and the reaction from Egypt on Page 2.

It was not known why the young man was so far north and on top of the mountain at the time of the fierce battle. It was also unknown how the Amalekite youth could have been captured, escape and travel the 100 miles from Mt. Gilboa to Ziklag in such a short time.

Knowledgeable sources reported that David was very distraught at the news of King Saul's death. David reportedly rent his garments, mourned, wept, and fasted during the day for Saul, Jonathan, and the soldiers of the Lord that had fallen by the sword.

Some sources were reportedly surprised by David's grief, given Saul's constant attempts to "nail" David, during on-again, off-again campaigns over the last few years and the speculation that David would most likely succeed Saul as king. Some suspected that the grief was mostly for Jonathan, David's friend and spiritual "brother," who David reportedly "loved more than any women."

During questioning, David asked the Amalekite youth, "How is it that you were not afraid to put forth your hand to desecrate the Lord's anointed?" David, unhappy with the Amalekite's response, apparently ordered one of his attendants to strike the boastful Amalekite man down. It was reported that David then said to the youth, "You are responsible for your own death, for you testified against yourself when you said, 'I dispatched the Lord's anointed.'"

It should be noted that the details in this report differ from the account of Saul's armor-bearer who had reported earlier that a wounded Saul had killed himself by falling on his own sword. Some scribes quietly but angrily complained to the press assembled here in Ziklag about David's hasty execution of the Amalekite youth. They said that it would now be impossible for them to determine which of the two accounts should be recorded for posterity.

The Cover Photographs

Front Cover: The photograph was taken at the Holy Family Shrine near Gretna, Nebraska. In my mind, this photograph represents salvation history, and the characters that play – and have played – a role in that history.

Stretch your imagination and think of every flower and blade of grass in the photograph as a character in salvation history. You will note that some of the characters – especially the big yellow flower in full bloom – are more prominent than others. In a sense that big yellow flower in full bloom and the similar flowers in the background represent the major biblical characters that I prayed and wrote about in this book – from Abraham to Saint Paul. The unidentifiable flowers, grass blades, and weeds in the background represent the lesser bit players in salvation history like Uzzah (Chapter 2), me, and you.

I was disappointed when I pulled this picture up on my computer and noticed that the big yellow flower was out-of-focus. I was tempted to look for an alternative photograph until I recalled that some of the major characters that I wrote about in this book, such as Joshua (Chapter 4) and Daniel (Chapter 5) were also a little fuzzy. So when you read about Joshua and Daniel in this book, think about the big fuzzy yellow flower on the front cover.

Back Cover: The grounds at the Holy Family Shrine change with the seasons. The three photographs on the back cover depict some of those changes:

The **top photograph** was taken in the spring before the annual and perennial flowers fully bloomed. Pay particular attention to the glass etching on the chapel window. It depicts the Holy Family – the biblical characters that I prayed and wrote about in Chapter 6 (A Nativity Prayer).

The **middle photograph** was taken after a heavy winter storm had filled the grotto between the visitor center and the chapel with a foot or so of snow. A statue of Mary (whom I wrote about in two of this book's chapters) is visible on the left. The sitting benches to the right are buried in the snow, not yet dug out.

The **bottom photograph** was taken during the fall of 2013, when a "controlled burn" took place on most of the shrine's 23 acres. The volunteer fire departments from Gretna and Louisville, Nebraska, used their expertise to burn off the unwanted weeds, burn up the unwanted wood ticks, and generally improve the long-term health of the native grasses that cover the property. I will resist the temptation to discuss the theological aspects of such controlled burns.

With that being said, let us start out with one of the stars of the Pentateuch and the faith that Abraham modeled for us.

Chapter 1

"Abraham's Faith" Prayer

Prayer	Vs.	Inspiration
Lord, God, creator of heaven and earth,	A1	Gn 14:18-20
Abram was righteous. He put his **faith** in you.	A2	Gn 15:6
You were his shield and he feared not! You made his reward very great.	A3	Gn 15:1
You blessed him in every way.	A4	Gn 24:1
You redeemed him.	A5	Is 29:22
Lord, God the Almighty, Abraham walked in your presence and was blameless.	B1	Gn 17:1
By **faith** Abraham obeyed, by **faith** he sojourned in the promised land, by **faith** he fathered Isaac.	B2	Heb 11:8-11
He was empowered by **faith** and gave glory to God.	B3	Rom 4:16-21
Lord, God of Vision,	C1	Gn 16:13
You made Sarah laugh. Nothing is too marvelous for the Lord to do.	C2	Gn 18:13-14
On her account all went well.	C3	Gn 12:16
You blessed Sarah and gave her a son.	C4	Gn 17:15-16
You provided the sheep for the holocaust.	C5	Gn 22:8
Lord, God Most High	D1	Gn 14:22
You put Abraham to the test, and he was "ready."	D2	Gn 22:1
Wisdom preserved him resolute – against pity for his child.	D3	Wis 10:5
You blessed him abundantly because he obeyed your command. His descendents are as countless as the stars in the sky. They possess the gates of their enemies. All the nations of the earth are blessed.	D4	Gn 22:15-18
He saw your day and rejoiced.	D5	John 8:56
O Lord, God of our father Abraham, direct my heart towards you.	E1	1 Chr 29:18
Do not take away your mercy from me, for the sake of Abraham, your beloved.	E2	Dn 3:35-36
Do not hide from me – instead single me out.	E3	Gn 18:17-19
Do not sweep me away.	E4	Gn 18:23
I have **faith**; I believe; I am a child of Abraham.	E5	Gal 3:6-9

Background

In Genesis 11:26 (after the creation, the fall, the flood, and the tower of Babel), we are introduced to a man named Abram. For the next fourteen chapters we learn much about the man that God selects to be our spiritual father. His name is changed from Abram to Abraham in Genesis 17:5 and his death is noted in Genesis 25:8. In between we read about these milestones:

- his relocation from Mesopotamia to the "promised land,"
- his temporary relocation to Egypt during a famine,
- his wife Sarai (Sarah),
- his relationship with Lot, his nephew,
- his military successes (Chapter 14),
- the birth of his sons (Isaac and Ishmael),
- the destruction of Sodom and Gomorrah,
- God's test of Abraham (to offer Isaac as holocaust), and
- much much more – but most importantly
- the covenant that God makes with Abraham (Chapters 15 and 17).

In fourteen or so chapters from Genesis, we learn why the name "Abraham" and the word "faith" are linked. It seemed appropriate to write a prayer about this "biblical biggie" – "the father of a host of nations" – and the faith that Abraham demonstrated for us. That prayer, that man, and that faith are the topic of this chapter.

"Abraham's Faith" Prayer - How is it Structured?

Let's take a look at this prayer. How is it structured? What are some of the key components of the prayer?

Overview

The initial inspirational verses all came from chapters 12 - 24 of Genesis. A computer search for "Abraham" brought forth a second set of verses from the rest of the Bible.

The prayer is divided into five sections. Each section starts with a different title for the Lord. All the titles used are found in the inspirational verses cited. The prayer sections are, for the most part, in chronological order (e.g., the covenant, the birth of Isaac, Abraham's test).

Faith is the major theological theme. The word **"faith"** is found six times in the printed prayer (as emphasized by the bold font).

I will go over the prayer, verse-by-verse, and then write a little at the end of the chapter on the *theology of faith* and a couple of other Abraham-related issues.

Verse by Verse

A1	Lord, God, creator of heaven and earth,

In the Bible passage below, Melchizedek, the king of Salem (Jerusalem?) blesses Abram with a reference to "**God** Most High" – the "**creator of heaven and earth**."

Every time we recite *The Apostles' Creed*, we say those words: *"I believe in **God**, the Father almighty, **creator of heaven and earth**."*

The Apostles' Creed is so called because it is:
- rightly considered to be a faithful summary of the apostles' faith,
- the ancient baptismal symbol of the Church of Rome, and
- the creed of the Roman Church, the See of Saint Peter (cf. CCC 194).

The Nicene Creed has a similar beginning: *"We believe in one **God**, the Father, the Almighty, **maker of heaven and earth**, of all that is, seen and unseen."*

Thus my prayer starts by addressing the Lord in a manner consistent with the great creeds of the Church.

Melchizedek is a mysterious figure. He pops up in Genesis 14 and then nothing else is heard of him in the Old Testament, except for a brief reference in Psalm 110. From these sources, the author of Hebrews develops the theology of Christ's priesthood. I will write more about Melchizedek, his relationship with Abraham, and his "priestly" relationship to Jesus at the end of this chapter.

Genesis 14:18-20: Melchizedek, king of Salem, brought out bread and wine, and being a priest of God Most High, he blessed Abram with these words: "Blessed be Abram by **God** Most High, the **creator of heaven and earth**; And blessed be God Most High, who delivered your foes into your hand." Then Abram gave him a tenth of everything.

A2	Abram was righteous. He put his faith in you.

Genesis 15:6 is among the most quoted Old Testament verses on faith, and the subject of much controversy amongst the Christian churches. The prayer verse above and the inspirational verse below flip-flop the order of events, but the facts noted are the same.

We note that Abraham is still Abram at this time. The Lord has not yet changed his name. His name will change when his role in salvation history changes. What is the nature of the "faith" that Abram displayed and why was it "credited" to him as "righteousness"? I will discuss these questions more in the "Theology of Faith" section of this chapter.

Genesis 15:6 - Abram put his **faith** in the LORD, who credited it to him as an act of righteousness.

A3	You were his shield and he feared not! You made his reward very great.
	God did many things for Abram. In Genesis 13, the Lord had Abram gaze to the north, south, east, and west to the lands in Canaan that the Lord gave him. In Genesis 14, Abram rescued his kinsman Lot and was blessed by Melchizedek, the king of Salem. After these events, the Lord instructed Abram to, "fear not." The Lord would continue to be his shield and reward him greatly. This prayer verse and the two that follow, acknowledge the blessings and the rewards that the Lord gave to Abram.
	Genesis 15:1 - Some time after these events, this word of the LORD came to Abram in a vision: "Fear not, Abram! I am your shield; I will make your reward very great."

A4	You blessed him in every way.
	As Abraham reached the end of his life, his relationship with the Lord was summarized. Scripture tells us that the Lord had blessed him in **every** way. From Scripture we can also deduce that Abraham's life was not necessarily easy. It was not a walk in the park – but it was blessed in **every** way. It was the "great reward" promised in the previous verse.
	Genesis 24:1 - Abraham had now reached a ripe old age, and the LORD had blessed him in every way.

A5	You redeemed him.
	"Redeemed" is a word we normally associate with Jesus but, as the prophet Isaiah notes in the inspirational verse below, God the Father also "redeemed." When and how did God the Father redeem Abraham? Was it at the time of the covenant? Was it after Abraham passed a test? The New American Bible, in the note for Isaiah 29:22, suggests that God redeemed Abraham "by freeing him from the idolatry of his native land." If this is the case, Abraham was redeemed before the covenant, before circumcision, and before God instructed him to sacrifice his son Isaac in a holocaust.
	Isaiah 29:22 - Therefore thus says the LORD, the **God** of the house of Jacob, who **redeemed Abraham**: Now Jacob shall have nothing to be ashamed of, nor shall his face grow pale.

B1	Lord, God the Almighty, Abraham walked in your presence and was blameless.

When the Lord reappeared to discuss the "covenant of circumcision" with Abram, the Lord reintroduced himself as "I am God the Almighty." Accordingly, this phrase is used to address God in this section of my prayer.

In the inspirational verse below (Gn 17:1), the last sentence is presented in the form of an instruction from "God the Almighty" to "Abram." In the prayer verse above, the context is changed from "instruction" to "mission accomplished."

A short time later (Gn 17:5), the Lord changed Abram's name to **Abraham**, "for I am making you the father of a host of nations." Abraham's role in salvation history is expanded as his name is expanded. Names were important to the Israelites. To some extent, an individual's name defined the person. So accordingly, the name used in the above prayer verse was also changed from Abram to Abraham, to acknowledge the new role that God announced in Genesis 17.

The Church (CCC 203) tells us: "God revealed himself to his people Israel by making his name known to them. A name expresses a person's essence and identity and the meaning of this person's life. God has a name; he is not an anonymous force. To disclose one's name is to make oneself known to others; in a way it is to hand oneself over by becoming accessible, capable of being known more intimately and address personally."

Accordingly, we can address "God the Almighty," and "Abraham," more intimately and personally. They are accessible to us. We know their essence and identity.

Genesis 17:1 - When Abram was ninety-nine years old, the LORD appeared to him and said: "I am **God the Almighty**. Walk in my presence and be blameless."

B2	By faith Abraham obeyed, by faith he sojourned in the promised land, by faith he fathered Isaac.

The author of Hebrews emphasizes the faith of Abraham. Each of the lines above stresses Abraham's faith. The first line is the key – **by faith Abraham obeyed.**

Hebrews 11:8-11: By faith Abraham obeyed when he was called to go out to a place that he was to receive as an inheritance; he went out, not knowing where he was to go. By faith he sojourned in the promised land as in a foreign country, … By faith he received power to generate, even though he was past the normal age – and Sarah herself was sterile – for he thought that the one who had made the promise was trustworthy.

B3	He was empowered by faith and gave glory to God.

The above prayer verse is a direct quote from Saint Paul's letter to the Romans. Saint Paul tells us that Abraham was empowered by faith. The inspirational verse below provides us with some additional information about faith.

Faith is a gift. The Church (CCC 153) tells us that: "*Faith is a gift of God, a supernatural virtue infused by him.*" The Church also states that before this faith can be exercised, man must also have God's help, the grace of God to move and assist him (cf. CCC 153).

The last sentence reminds me of the two-part epoxy glues that work so great when properly mixed. You may be familiar with these products. Part A (faith) does not work until it is mixed with Part B (grace). Neither part will work alone. Mr. Handy Mann says, "I have used two-part epoxy glues before. I have faith that they will work as advertised. I am fully convinced that if I mix Part A and Part B properly, it will do what it is guaranteed to do."

Doesn't Mr. Handy Mann's product testimonial sound like what the *Catechism* (CCC 153) notes above?

Romans 4:16-21: For this reason, it depends on **faith**, so that it may be **a gift**, and the promise may be guaranteed to all his descendants, not to those who only adhere to the law but to those who follow the faith of Abraham, ... **he was empowered by faith and gave glory to God** and was fully convinced that what he had promised he was also able to do.

C1	Lord, God of Vision,

This section of the prayer (C1 - C5) concerns two of the women in Abraham's life, his wife Sarah (the mother of Isaac) and Hagar (Sarah's maid, Abraham's concubine, and Ishmael's mother – by Abraham).

Genesis 16:6-14 tells us that the pregnant Hagar ran away because Sarah was abusing her. The Lord's messenger found her in the wilderness and Instructed her to return to Sarah. The Lord's messenger also instructed Hagar to name her son-to-be "Ishmael."
At this point in the narrative, Hagar spoke the verse (Gn 16:13) printed below.

In the prayer verse above, I address the Lord with the same phrase ("God of Vision") that Hagar used. Note the question that Hagar asks in Genesis 16:13, "*Have I really seen God and remained alive after my vision?*"

Most of us have not seen God, or, if we have, we have not recognized him. We look forward to seeing God (the beatific vision) after we die. The Church (CCC 163) tells us: "Faith makes us taste in advance [before we die] the light of the **beatific vision**, the goal of our journey here below. ... **So faith is already the beginning of eternal life**: .... "

Genesis 16:13 - To the **LORD** who spoke to her she gave a name, saying, "You are the **God of Vision**"; she meant, "Have I really seen God and remained alive after my vision?"

C2	You made Sarah laugh. Nothing is too marvelous for the Lord to do.

Isn't this verse **marvelous**? It is my favorite verse in the prayer. The Lord recognizes how preposterous his words might sound to an elderly woman. Sarah was advanced in age when God promised Abraham that his descendents would be countless. While the Lord can appreciate why Sarah might laugh at the news of a possible pregnancy, he must also remind Abraham that he can and does **marvelous** things. In this case the Lord had the last laugh (when Isaac was born).

The Church (CCC 156) reminds us: "What moves us to believe is not the fact that revealed truths appear as true and intelligible in the light of our natural reason." Sarah's natural reason told her that she would bear no children. We should believe because of the authority of God, who can neither deceive nor be deceived (cf. CCC 156).

Genesis 18:13-14: But the LORD said to Abraham: "Why did Sarah laugh and say, 'Shall I really bear a child, old as I am?' Is anything too **marvelous** for the LORD to do? At the appointed time, about this time next year, I will return to you, and Sarah will have a son."

C3	On her account all went well.

Abraham is another example of the imperfect humans that the Lord has dealt with over the ages. Twice in Genesis (12:10-20 and 20:1-18), Abraham told others that Sarah was his "sister," rather than his "wife." In both instances, Abraham profited. In the verse below we read of the animals that Abraham received while he was in Egypt and Sarah (his sister) was in the Pharaoh's palace.

Genesis 12:16 - On her account it went very well with Abram, and he received flocks and herds, male and female slaves, male and female asses, and camels.

C4	You blessed Sarah and gave her a son.

While the previous prayer verse (C3) reflects the "material wellness" that Sarah provided, we must remember that God blessed her and gave her a son.

Genesis 17:15-16: God further said to Abraham: "As for your wife Sarai, do not call her Sarai; her name shall be Sarah. I will bless her, and I will give you a son by her. Him also will I bless; he shall give rise to nations, and rulers of peoples shall issue from him."

C5	You provided the sheep for the holocaust.

This prayer verse connects the "son" reference in the previous verse with a later verse in Genesis about that son. Until the angel interceded, Sarah's son, Isaac, was the sheep for the holocaust.

In this verse from Genesis, Abraham, once again, demonstrates his **faith** in God.

The Church (CCC 2572) notes that, "Abraham's **faith** does not weaken ... for he 'considered that God was able to raise men even from the dead.' And so the father of believers [Abraham] is conformed to the likeness of the Father who will not spare his own Son but will deliver him up for us all. Prayer restores man to God's likeness and enables him to share in the power of God's love that saves the multitude."

Genesis 22:8 - "Son," Abraham answered, "God himself will provide the sheep for the holocaust." Then the two continued going forward.

D1	Lord, God Most High

The fourth section of the prayer (D1 - D5) focuses on Abraham and the major test that the Lord gave him. The prayer reverts to the story of Melchizedek in Genesis 14 to find a fitting way to address the Lord. In Genesis 14, both Abraham and Melchizedek (a Gentile) referred to the "God Most High."

Genesis 14:22 - But Abram replied to the king of Sodom: "I have sworn to the **LORD, God Most High**, the creator of heaven and earth,

D2	You put Abraham to the test, and he was "ready."

What a test and what a response. After Adam was tested he hid (Gn 3:8). Abraham was not going to hide after his test; he was "ready."

The Church (CCC 164 and 144) notes that, "faith is often lived in darkness and can be put to the **test**. ... To obey ... in faith is to submit freely to the word that has been heard, because its truth is guaranteed by God, who is Truth itself. **Abraham is the model** of such obedience offered us by Sacred Scripture."

Genesis 22:1 - Some time after these events, God put Abraham to the test. He called to him, "Abraham!" "Ready!" he replied.

D3	Wisdom preserved him resolute – against pity for his child.

When I used my computer to search for "Abraham," a verse from the book of Wisdom popped up. If you look at that verse below, you will not find the word "Abraham" (nor the word "wisdom" for that matter). I discovered, after further investigation, that Wisdom 10:5 was displayed because of a reference to Abraham in the "notes" section of my Bible.

The "wisdom" of the verse is that Abraham did not allow a short-term pity for his son to interfere with God's long-term plan for Isaac. Abraham was resolute; his actions were firm; he did not waiver. We can only imagine what thoughts were going through Abraham's mind, but wisdom carried him forward.

Wisdom is often referenced in feminine terms. The prayer verse thus makes a substitution, and "She" becomes "Wisdom." With that substitution, the prayer verse above becomes almost a direct quote from the book of Wisdom.

Wisdom 10:5 - She, when the nations were sunk in universal wickedness, knew the just man, kept him blameless before God, and **preserved him resolute against pity for his child.**

D4	**You blessed him abundantly because he obeyed your command.** **His descendents are as countless as the stars in the sky.** **They possess the gates of their enemies.** **All the nations of the earth are blessed.**

This prayer verse lists all the good things that happened to Abraham because he **obeyed**.

The Church (cf. CCC 706) notes that:

- God promises descendants to Abraham, as the fruit of faith and of the power of the Holy Spirit. In Abraham's progeny all the nations of the earth will be blessed.

- Abraham's progeny will be Christ himself, in whom the outpouring of the Holy Spirit will "gather into one the children of God who are scattered abroad."

- God commits himself by his own solemn oath to giving his beloved Son and the promised Holy Spirit, who is the guarantee of our inheritance until we acquire possession of it.

Genesis 22:15-18: Again the LORD'S messenger called to Abraham from heaven and said: "I swear by myself, declares the LORD, that because you acted as you did in not withholding from me your beloved son, I will bless you abundantly and make your descendants as countless as the stars of the sky and the sands of the seashore; your descendants shall take possession of the gates of their enemies, and in your descendants all the nations of the earth shall find blessing – all this because you **obeyed** my command."

D5	He saw your day and rejoiced.

This prayer verse is inspired by the "good news" noted in the Gospel of John. The New American Bible note regarding this verse suggests that Abraham saw "it" – the birth of Isaac – as the beginning of the fulfillment of the promises that God had given him concerning his progeny. After he saw baby Isaac he rejoiced and was glad.

John 8:56 - [Jesus answered:] Abraham your father rejoiced to see my day; he saw it and was glad.

E1	O Lord, God of our father Abraham, direct my heart towards you.

The last section of the prayer (E1 - E5) becomes a personal petition. The Lord is addressed as the God of "our" father, Abraham. The personal tone of this section continues in the second line of the verse. I petition God to direct my heart towards him (i.e., provide me with grace and faith).

1 Chronicles 29:18 - O LORD, God of our fathers Abraham, Isaac, and Israel, keep such thoughts in the hearts and minds of your people forever, and direct their hearts toward you.

E2	Do not take away your mercy from me, for the sake of Abraham, your beloved.

This prayer verse is almost a direct quote from the book of Daniel. The (deuterocanonical) verses[4] below were prayed by Azariah[5] (more familiar as Abednego – his Babylonian name) as he walked about in the flames of the fire that King Nebuchadnezzar had ordered set to burn him to death. God heard his prayer and he was unharmed.

Daniel 3:35-36: Do not take away your mercy from us, for the sake of Abraham, your beloved, Isaac your servant, and Israel your holy one, to whom you promised to multiply their offspring like the stars of heaven, or the sand on the shore of the sea.

E3	Do not hide from me – instead single me out.

Genesis 18 provides us with another marvelous story about Abraham's hospitality and his concern for the innocent among us. In **Genesis 18:16-33**, the Lord reflects on his decision to destroy Sodom and Gomorrah. The Lord, in the inspirational verses cited below, reflects on whether he should tell Abraham what he intends to do to these cities.

Genesis 18:17-19: The LORD reflected: "**Shall I hide from Abraham** what I am about to do, now that he is to become a great and populous nation, and all the nations of the earth are to find blessing in him? Indeed, **I have singled him out** that he may direct his sons and his posterity to keep the way of the LORD by doing what is right and just, so that the LORD may carry into effect for Abraham the promises he made about him."

E4	Do not sweep me away.
During Abraham's discussion with the Lord concerning the innocent that reside in Sodom, Abraham asks the Lord, "Will you sweep away the innocent with the guilty?" Don't you love the imagery of those words? Can't you just visualize a giant Lord with a giant broom just sweeping away the guilty (and innocent?) citizens of Sodom?	
Genesis 18:23 - Then Abraham drew nearer to him and said: "Will you sweep away the innocent with the guilty?	

E5	I have faith; I believe; I am a child of Abraham.
The prayer ends with three statements of faith that were inspired by several verses from Paul's letter to the Galatians. We have traveled a long way with Abraham via this prayer. With the help of Saint Paul, we return to Genesis 15:6, "*Abram put his faith in the Lord, who credited it to him as an act of righteousness.*" Catholics profess their faith – their beliefs – in creeds (e.g., *The Apostle's Creed, The Nicene Creed*). The word "creed" is derived from the Latin word *credo, which* means, "I believe." **I have faith – I believe** the words written in our creeds. In Galatians, Paul states that those who have faith, those who believe, are children of God. The prayer concludes, accordingly.	
Galatians 3:6-9: Thus Abraham "believed God, and it was credited to him as righteousness." Realize then that **it is those who have faith who are children of Abraham**. Scripture, which saw in advance that God would justify the Gentiles by faith, foretold the good news to Abraham, saying, "Through you shall all the nations be blessed." Consequently, those who have faith are blessed along with Abraham who had faith.	

Theology of Faith

As the prayer was reviewed, verse by verse, I discussed several of the Church's teachings on faith – the faith that Abraham demonstrated. I will not dwell on the topic to a great extent, except to cite two more paragraphs from the *Catechism*.

The Church (CCC 143) teaches: "*By faith*, man completely submits his intellect and his will to God. With his whole being man gives his assent to God the revealer. Sacred Scripture calls this human response to God, the author of revelation, 'the obedience of faith.'"

The Church (CCC 1814) teaches: "Faith is the theological virtue by which we believe in God and believe all that he has said and revealed to us, and that Holy Church proposes for our belief, because he is truth itself."

Theology - Abraham and Melchizedek

As I noted previously, the fourteenth chapter of Genesis tells us about Abram the military leader, his successes on the battlefield and his subsequent meeting with Melchizedek, the king of Salem and priest of the God Most High.

Genesis 14 is unlike any other chapter in Genesis. Indeed, if you skipped from Genesis 13 to Genesis 15, you probably wouldn't notice that it was missing. The obvious question then becomes, why does Genesis 14 exist and what is God trying to tell us? The secondary question is, who is this Melchizedek fellow and what does God want us to know about him?

I don't intend to spend much time on Melchizedek because the theology of Melchizedek is complicated and he is not the focus of this prayer, as are Abraham and faith. But since Genesis 14 entwines Melchizedek and Abram, I will write a little bit about him.

Here is what the Old Testament says about Melchizedek:

> When Abram returned from his victory… **Melchizedek**, king of Salem, brought out bread and wine, and being a priest of God Most High, he blessed Abram with these word: "Blessed be Abram by God Most High, the creator of heaven and earth; And blessed be God Most High, who delivered your foes into your hand." Then Abram gave him a tenth of everything. – Gn 14:17-20

> The LORD has sworn and will not waver: "**Like Melchizedek you are a priest forever.**" At your right hand is the Lord, who crushes kings on the day of wrath, who, robed in splendor, judges nations, crushes heads across the wide earth, who drinks from the brook by the wayside and thus holds high the head. – Ps 110:4-7

That's basically it.

From the Old Testament we thus learn the following about Melchizedek:

- He was the king of Salem (traditionally identified with Jerusalem).[6]
- He brought out bread and wine to Abram when Abram returned victorious.
- He was also a priest of "God Most High" (a Canaanite priest).[7]
- He blessed Abram by "God Most High, the creator of heaven and earth."
- He blessed God Most High (who delivered Abram's foes).
- He received a tenth of everything from Abram (the priestly portion).[8]
- He was a priest forever.

Theology - Abraham and Melchizedek (continued)

Why would the victorious Abram tithe a stranger, a gentile priest? The answer to that question is developed in the New Testament, in Hebrews 5-7. If you wish, you can read those chapters yourself. I will stop here, except to cite three paragraphs from the *Catechism* that refer directly to Melchizedek. Note first, however, that Abraham, our faithful and spiritual father saw something in Melchizedek – some connection – that he honored. The Church teaches:

- "The Bible venerates several great figures among the Gentiles [including] … the king-priest Melchizedek – a figure of Christ" … (CCC 58).

- "Everything that the priesthood of the Old Covenant prefigured finds its fulfillment in Christ Jesus, the 'one mediator between God and men.' The Christian tradition considers Melchizedek, 'priest of God Most High,' as a prefiguration of the priesthood of Christ, the unique 'high priest after the order of Melchizedek' …" (CCC 1544).

- **"The Church sees in the gesture of the king-priest Melchizedek, who 'brought out bread and wine,' a prefiguring of her own offering"** (CCC 1333).

As noted previously, none of the information in Genesis 14 was required to understand the chapters that preceded it, nor the chapters that followed it. We must note, however, that Genesis 14 **was** placed between chapters 13 and 15. There must be something in that chapter concerning God's plan for our salvation.

If the meeting of Abram and Melchizedek was not in Genesis 14:
- there may not have been a Psalm 110,
- there would be no theology to develop in Hebrews 5-7, and
- we would not understand the priestly function of Jesus, as well as we do.

What do you think; **was** Melchizedek a major or minor character in salvation history?

Theology - Faith and Works

> *He took him outside and said, "Look up at the sky and count the stars, if you can. Just so," he added, "shall your descendants be." Abram put his faith in the LORD, who credited it to him as an act of righteousness. – Genesis 15:5-6*

Christians have disagreed for centuries, at least since the Reformation, about whether anything besides the faith that Abraham demonstrated above is required for us to attain salvation. St. Paul (e.g., Romans 4) and St. James (James 2) are often cited during these "discussions." St. Paul, the apparent champion of "faith," is pitted against Saint James, the apparent champion of "good works." Both sides line up with their favorite verses and the verse slinging begins:

> *Indeed, if Abraham was justified on the basis of his works, he has reason to boast; but this was not so in the sight of God. For what does the scripture say? "Abraham believed God, and it was credited to him as righteousness." – Romans 4:2-3*

> *It was not through the law that the promise was made to Abraham and his descendants that he would inherit the world, but through the righteousness that comes from faith. – Romans 4:13*

> *What good is it, my brothers, if someone says he has faith but does not have works? Can that faith save him? – James 2:14*

> *So also faith of itself, if it does not have works, is dead. – James 2:17*

> *See how a person is justified by works and not by **faith alone**. – James 2:24*

A disinterested party might ask how the Bible could say such completely different things. The short answer is that these two chapters do not disagree. They just stress different aspects of the same situation. Semantics – the structure, development, meaning and context of words – has always been a factor in the discussion of faith and works.

You may remember the commotion that occurred towards the end of 1999 when the Catholic Church and the Lutheran World Federation issued the *Joint Declaration on the Doctrine of Justification.* That document was one attempt to find some common "semantic" ground.

Theology - Faith and Works (continued)

Much has been written over the centuries about this issue. For this reason and because my main goals in this chapter are Abraham, faith, and prayer, I am not going to delve into this issue to any extent.

If you are interested in the topic, I would recommend that you read *The Salvation Controversy*, by James Akin.[9] Akin does an excellent job of examining this topic from both Catholic and Protestant perspectives.

Akin notes in his book that Saint Paul's point in Romans 4 (and throughout his letters) was that man was not saved by "*erga nomou*", "works of the Torah" or "works of Law" – versus the "good works" that one does because of a belief in Jesus' message.[10]

I believe that Saint Paul, in Romans, was telling the "Christians" in Rome, that they **would not or could not** be "justified" by rigorously attempting to obey all the sabbath, circumcision, and dietary laws ("works of Torah"). We need to remember that by the time of Saint Paul, the "works of Torah" were extensive.

I believe that Saint Paul was telling the "Christians" in Rome to develop and focus their faith on the Trinitarian God and the good news that Jesus brought to the earth, which over time would naturally result in "good works." Saint Paul's thoughts on "good works" (versus "works of Torah") are better expressed in the quotation from Romans noted below:

> By your stubbornness and impenitent heart, you are storing up wrath for yourself for the day of wrath and revelation of the just judgment of God, who will repay everyone according to his **works**: eternal life to those who seek glory, honor, and immortality through perseverance in **good works**, but wrath and fury to those who selfishly disobey the truth and obey wickedness. – Romans 2:5-8

Akins notes in his book that, "the expression 'faith alone' (Greek, *pisteos monon*) appears only once in the Bible – in James 2:24 – where it is rejected."[11] Akins goes on to write, "James *does not see anything wrong* with the faith he is talking about. The *faith* isn't the problem; it's being *alone* is the problem."[12]

The Church (CCC 1815) teaches: "The gift of faith remains in one who has not sinned against it. But 'faith apart from works is dead': when it is deprived of hope and love, faith does not fully unite the believer to Christ and does not make him a living member of his Body."

Returning to Abraham and his faith, we should not forget or ignore the "good works" that Abraham did. Reread Genesis 18 and note the nature of the hospitality and good works that Abraham undertook for his three visitors.

Catechism Check?

I believe that the prayer in this chapter is consistent with the *Catechism of the Catholic Church*.

As you should have noted by now, the *Catechism* was referenced multiple times in this chapter on Abraham and faith.

Coincidentally the *Catechism* itself is organized around **faith**. The Church (cf. CCC 13) notes that the *Catechism* itself is supported by four pillars:

- the baptismal profession of **faith** (the *Creed*),
- the sacraments of **faith**,
- the life of **faith** (the *Commandments*), and
- the prayer of the **believe**r (the *Lord's Prayer*).

To begin my research, I first referred to the *Subject Index* listings for:
- Faith, and
- Faith, profession of

At later times, I referred to the *Index of Citations* in the back of the *Catechism* for the paragraphs that were cited in Genesis 12-24, and the other verses that inspired the prayer.

We Can Pray

Abraham provides us with an excellent example of "faith in action." He **led** his family through much of the Mideast. He **interceded** for the innocent and led an army to protect his family.

Abraham had faith and was "ready" when he was put to the ultimate test.
Are we or will we be "ready" when we are tested?

I have found it interesting during my time on this earth that I have seen so many:
- Catholics – who appreciate the need for "good works" – do so few, and
- Protestants – who deny the need for "good works" – do so many.

Isn't our faith interesting at times?

Will Christians ever jointly declare one doctrine on justification and concentrate our efforts to do the "good works" that St. Paul and St. James wrote about?

We can pray – we can at least start with prayer!

Chapter 2

An "Exodus" Prayer

Prayer	Vs.	Inspiration
Lord, God the Almighty,	A1	Ex 6:2
receive glory through me.	A2	Ex 14:17
In your mercy, you led the people you redeemed; In your strength, you guided them to your holy dwelling.	B1	Ex 15:13
In the morning and evening twilight, you fed them.	B2	Ex 16:11-12
You spared them, showed them your power, and made your name resound throughout the earth.	B3	Ex 9:16
Be with me, as you were with Moses.	C1	Ex 3:12
Do not make me obstinate, as you made the Pharaoh.	C2	Ex 7:3-4
Do not let me become hardhearted, when the thunder and hail in my life ceases.	C3	Ex 9:34-35
Provide me with a staff, like you provided Moses.	D1	Ex 4:17
Assist me as I speak, as you assisted Aaron.	D2	Ex 4:10-16
Be my God! Take me as one of your own.	D3	Ex 6:7
If you please, Lord, send me!	D4	Ex 4:13
The Lord is my banner.	E1	Ex 17:15-16
My strength and my courage is the Lord. He has been my savior. He is my God and I praise him.	E2	Ex 15:1-3
The Lord shall reign forever and ever.	E3	Ex 15:18

Background

The prayer in this chapter may look familiar. You might have seen this prayer in the introduction to my first book *A Catholic Prays Scripture: and tips for how you can too*. In that book I noted that this prayer was the first prayer that I ever wrote and described the circumstances that lead to my process for "praying scripture." I won't repeat those details, except to note that I wrote the prayer in response to the following Bible study optional challenge:

> *Write a prayer or song or poem or do some art work that expresses something of the meaning of Exodus, chapters one through eighteen.*[13]

While I included this prayer in the introduction to my first book, I didn't at that time "flesh out" the prayer verses, develop any of the theology in the prayer, or discuss any of the "biblical biggies" (e.g., Moses, Aaron, the Pharaoh) noted in the prayer. That is what I will attempt to do in this chapter.

While this prayer was the first prayer I ever wrote, this chapter wasn't. This chapter was one of the last chapters (of the four-volume series) that I wrote after I decided to include a chapter on Moses in this book.

I decided that no book on "biblical biggies" would be complete without a chapter on Moses. "In Israelite tradition Moses was simply the founder of Israel, and no lesser designation does justice to the place he occupies. ... He is the founder of Yahwism, the worship of Yahweh as the God of Israel. ... Moses is the mediator of the covenant."[14]

While this chapter will focus for the most part on Moses, the prayer itself (given the optional challenge) was focused on the first eighteen (of forty) chapters of Exodus. So let me start with a brief outline of those eighteen chapters:

Chapter (verses)	Main Topic [15]
1	The oppression of the Hebrews in Egypt
2	The birth and early career of Moses
3 – 4	The vocation of Moses
(5:1 – 6:1)	Moses before the Pharaoh
(6:2 – 7:7)	A second account of Moses' vocation and appearance before the Pharaoh
(7:8 – 12:28)	The ten plagues of Egypt (water turned into blood, frogs, gnats, flies, pestilence, boils, hail, locusts, darkness, and the death of firstborn sons)
(12:29 – 15:21)	The departure from Egypt and the passage of the sea
(15:22 – 18:27)	From the sea to Sinai

As you can see from the preceding outline, the first eighteen chapters of Exodus describe Moses' early years: his birth, the vocation that God encouraged him to pursue, his interactions with the Pharaoh on behalf of his people, and the subsequent exodus from Egypt to the Sinai Peninsula – on the way to the Promised Land. Per the optional challenge, the prayer was limited to the first eighteen chapters of Exodus. In the rest of the chapter, however, I will attempt to provide a broader view of Moses' life and his role in salvation history.

Moses

As described in the Pentateuch, the first five books of the Old Testament, Moses was the **intermediary** between God and "His" people. The Hebrews were both "His" (God's) and "his" (Moses') people.

The phrase "The Lord said to Moses" appears 112 times in my Bible. The Lord spoke to Moses. Moses relayed the Lord's message to His people. As an intermediary, Moses also kept the Lord apprised of the condition of His people. In many instances God's people were grumbling and Moses passed the people's concerns back to the Lord.

If I had to pick one word to describe Moses' service for God and God's people, it would be perseverance:
- perseverance as he dealt with the Pharaoh,
- perseverance as a mediator between the Lord and His people, and
- perseverance during the desert sojourn to the Promised Land.

It is hard to think of Moses without thinking of the Ten Commandments and the law. Moses was not the lawgiver. God was the lawgiver. But, as an intermediary, Moses also became the mediator of the law for His people.

Moses, and his role in salvation history, was oft noted in the New Testament. The name "Moses" can be found in twelve of the New Testament books and in the New Testament he is often associated with the law. Two verses from the book of Acts summarize Moses' role in salvation history and the subsequent impact of Jesus on the law of Moses.

> *This Moses … God sent as (both) **ruler** and **deliverer**, through the angel who appeared to him in the bush. – Acts 7:35*

> *You must know, my brothers, that through [Jesus] forgiveness of sins is being proclaimed to you, (and) in regard to everything from which you could not be justified under **the law of Moses**, in him every believer is justified. – Acts 13:38-39*

More on Moses

It should be noted that Moses is not presented in Exodus as a "plaster saint," or in a consistent manner. He is presented at times with a certain diffidence which approached timidity.[16] Moses was a reluctant leader.

> *Now, Moses himself was by far the meekest man on the face of the earth. – Nm 12:3*

The meekest man on the face of the earth, however, could get frustrated and lose his temper at times, as recorded in the passages below.

> *On one occasion, after Moses had grown up, when he visited his kinsmen and witnessed their forced labor, he saw an Egyptian striking a Hebrew, one of his own kinsmen. Looking about and seeing no one, he slew the Egyptian and hid him in the sand. – Ex 2:11-12*
>
> *I [Moses] cannot carry all this people by myself, for they are too heavy for me. If this is the way you will deal with me, then please do me the favor of killing me at once, so that I need no longer face this distress. – Nm 11:14-15*

The Lord was not always pleased with the way that Moses acted.

> *On the journey, at a place where they spent the night, the Lord came upon Moses and would have killed him. But ... – Ex 4:24-25*

A discussion of Moses would not be complete without some comments on how God punished Moses for a fault that is not clearly delineated in the Bible. The punishment is noted in the verse below.

> *But the LORD said to Moses and Aaron, "Because you were not faithful to me in showing forth my sanctity before the Israelites, **you shall not lead this community into the land I will give them.**" – Nm 20:12*

And so it was. Aaron died sixteen verses later (Nm 20:28) and Moses died in the land of Moab, overlooking the Promised Land, as the Lord said (Dt 34:5).

Moses was certainly an interesting biblical character and deserves our consideration as we pray. Later in this chapter, I will also write about the Pharaoh, the major villain in Exodus. I will discuss why the Pharaoh, via his free will, chose to become obstinate, obdurate, and hard-hearted.

An "Exodus" Prayer - How is it Structured?

Let's take a look at this prayer. How is it structured? What are some of the key components of the prayer?

Overview

The prayer is divided into five sections (A-E). As usual, the prayer is a mixture of themes and types of prayer:

- The first section (A) is unusual in that it starts with a petition.

- The second section (B) is a mixture of wisdom (instruction) and thanksgiving.

- Sections C and D, while noting how the Lord blessed Moses and Aaron, also contain prayers of petition.

- The last section of the prayer (E) is adoration.

I have found that one of the hardest things to do, as regards "praying Scripture," is to come up with titles for the prayers. I always struggle with this task – trying to think of a short word or two to describe the nature of the prayer. This prayer was no exception. The title of this prayer reflects the "optional challenge" – to write a prayer based on the first eighteen chapters of Exodus.

The title of the prayer can, however, be viewed from another perspective.

- The first part of the prayer (A1 - B3) reflects Exodus (the book) – the story of how Moses led his people out of Egypt, through the desert, to the Promised Land.

- The next part of the prayer (C1 - D4) is a petition to the Lord concerning my personal exodus, through my spiritual desert to the Lord's promised land. Like Moses, I can see the promised land on the horizon.

- The only questions remaining are if, how, and when I (the prayer) might enter the promised land. The prayer ends (E1 - E3) with adoration and thanksgiving for the Lord of the "Promised Land."

So let's start out and examine An "Exodus" Prayer - verse by verse.

Verse by Verse

A1	Lord, God the Almighty,

God tells Moses, "I am the Lord" – thus I address God accordingly. The first 18 chapters of Exodus confirm that he is almighty.

The title "Lord," is derived from the Hebrew word "Adonai," which distinguishes this divine title from the more general "my lord," which is used for human beings. The Hebrew base word signifies authority, the power to command. The title "Lord" also suggests God's Kingship. It is a solemn hymnic title, used most frequently in invocations.[17]

Exodus 6:2 - God also said to Moses, "I am the LORD."

A2	receive glory through me.

Let it suffice, for now, to note that the Lord receives glory through many people and many ways. The prayer verse above simply petitions the Lord to somehow receive glory through me (or the person praying the prayer).

Exodus 14:17 - But I [the LORD] will make the Egyptians so obstinate that they will go in after them. Then I will receive glory through Pharaoh and all his army, his chariots and charioteers.

B1	In your mercy, you led the people you redeemed; In your strength, you guided them to your holy dwelling.

This section (B1 - B3) reminds us of the many wonderful things that the Lord did for Moses and his chosen people and the wonderful things that he continues to do for us today.

The prayer verse above is a direct quote of the inspirational verse printed below. Many scriptural verses need no altering. You just need to fit them into the prayer, where and as appropriate. The commas were added to the prayer verse to emphasize God's mercy and strength when the prayer is read.

I will have a lot more to say about God's *hesed* – his mercy – later in this chapter.

Exodus 15:13 - In your **mercy** you led the people you redeemed; in your strength you guided them to your holy dwelling.

B2	In the morning and evening twilight, you fed them.

The prayer verse, in nine words, simplifies, for purposes of prayer, what is written in the forty-eight words in the inspirational passage below. It is important that we acknowledge in our prayers what God has done and continues to do for us. God does not need to be reminded that he fed his chosen people in the desert. We need to be reminded of what he did and continues to do for us.

The Lord started with the basics. He fed his chosen people manna in the morning and quail at night. Note that the grumbling had already begun. I will return to this grumbling, this murmuring, later. It was not a one-of-a-kind event. It was, and is, how mankind oft responds to the Lord, our God. It continues to this day.

Exodus 16:11-12: The LORD spoke to Moses and said, "I have heard the grumbling of the Israelites. Tell them: In the evening twilight you shall eat flesh, and in the morning you shall have your fill of bread, so that you may know that I, the LORD, am your God."

B3	You spared them, showed them your power, and made your name resound throughout the earth.

The last verse of this section summarizes, why God did what he did. The words in the prayer verse are almost a direct quote. They were tweaked a bit to reflect the position of the person reading the prayer.

The prayer verse speaks of God's **power** and how he demonstrated it to his people. In Exodus, God tested his people (40 years in the desert) and he tested the Pharaoh (the plagues).

Exodus 9:16 - [Then the LORD told Moses:] "… this is why I have spared you: to show you my power and to make my name resound throughout the earth!"

C1	Be with me, as you were with Moses.

The prayer switches (C1 - C3) to personal petitions. The Lord, in the inspirational verse below, assured Moses that he would be with him – as "his" people were led out of Egypt. Jesus, at a later time, also assured the apostles that he would be with them as they went about their work on his behalf. The petition is a simple "ask and you shall receive" request that God be with me, as he was with Moses and the apostles.

Note the **"his"** in the first sentence above. Does it refer to God (i.e., God's people) or to Moses (i.e., Moses' people)? In this case it could apply to both God and Moses. They both demonstrated love and concern for their sometimes-disappointing people.

Exodus 3:12 - He [God] answered, "I will be with you; and this shall be your proof that it is I who have sent you: when you bring my people out of Egypt, you will worship God on this very mountain."

C2	Do not make me obstinate, as you made the Pharaoh.

The Pharaoh was obstinate. He stubbornly refused to allow Moses to lead God's people out of Egypt. Every so often, while the affect of a plague was fresh in his mind, he would recognize his sin – but he would soon stubbornly revert to sin.

Remember, as you read the book of Exodus and the remainder of this chapter, that the Pharaoh was more than a king or political leader. The Pharaoh was also considered to be a god. From that perspective, the dialog in the Bible reflects the actions of God and a human that claimed to be a god. The ten plagues thus represent an epic saga between good (God) and evil (Pharaoh, a false god).

This prayer verse petitions the Lord to prevent me (or the person praying the prayer) from becoming as obstinate as the Pharaoh was.

Exodus 7:3-4: Yet I [the LORD] will make Pharaoh so obstinate that, despite the many signs and wonders that I will work in the land of Egypt, he will not listen to you.

C3	Do not let me become hardhearted, when the thunder and hail in my life ceases.

This petition is a variation (i.e., "let me" versus "make me") of the previous prayer verse.

In the inspirational verse below, the word "obdurate" is used. Since obdurate is not a commonly used English word, I used the synonym "hardhearted" in the prayer verse. Hardhearted is a very graphic word. Can't you just see and feel a hard heart? The word certainly conveys an utterly unfeeling, pitiless, and cruel attitude.

Exodus 9:34-35: But Pharaoh, seeing that the rain and hail and thunder had ceased, sinned again: he with his servants became obdurate, and in his obstinacy he would not let the Israelites go, as the LORD had foretold through Moses.

D1	Provide me with a staff, like you provided Moses.

This section of the prayer (D1 - D4) contains four powerful petitions, four big-time requests.

You should really ask yourself, before praying the above verse, whether you "really" want this prayer answered. Do you really want "a staff" (i.e., the responsibility) that God gave Moses? If you read Exodus, you will note that even Moses did not want this kind of responsibility. Moses, in affect, argued with the Lord about whether the Lord had picked the right person for the job. In the end, I think that Moses recognized that he did meet the main criteria that the Lord had for the task at hand. Moses loved "his" people.

Exodus 4:17 - [Then the LORD became angry with Moses and said], "Take this staff in your hand; with it you are to perform the signs."

D2	Assist me as I speak, as you assisted Aaron.

The above petition is a very personal request from me. Public speaking is not my strength. For that matter, even a one-on-one "discussion" about God is not my strength. In this respect, I am like Moses. Note the exchange in the inspirational verse below between the Lord and Moses.

The Lord, though angry and frustrated with Moses, recognized that everyone was not given the same gifts. He matched Aaron with Moses – a spokesman and a leader – and sent them on their way. He later sent his apostles out in pairs to evangelize. The Lord recognizes our individual gifts and the cumulative power of the gifts given to the Church and all its members.

Note also that the Lord did not absolve Moses from any speaking assignments. First, Moses had to "speak" to Aaron about this matter. God was not going to handle this for him. Secondly, the Lord promised to assist "both you and him in speaking." In the prayer verse above, I ask for the same assistance that the Lord gave to Moses and Aaron.

Exodus 4:10-16: Moses, however, said to the LORD, "If you please, Lord, I have never been eloquent, neither in the past, nor recently, nor now that you have spoken to your servant; but I am slow of speech and tongue." … "If you please, Lord, send someone else!"

Then the LORD became angry with Moses and said, "Have you not your brother, **Aaron** the Levite? I know that he is an eloquent speaker. Besides, he is now on his way to meet you. When he sees you, his heart will be glad. You are to speak to him, then, and put the words in his mouth. **I will assist both you and him in speaking** and will teach the two of you what you are to do. He shall speak to the people for you: he shall be your spokesman, and you shall be as God to him.

D3	Be my God! Take me as one of your own.

The prayer verse transforms the words of the Lord to Moses. It becomes my petition.

Exodus 6:7 - [The LORD said], "I will take you as **my own** people, and you shall have me as **your God**. You will know that I, the LORD, am your God when I free you from the labor of the Egyptians

D4	If you please, Lord, send me!

The last verse in this section is also a reversal. In the inspirational verse below, Moses respectfully pleads with the Lord to "send someone else!" Note the explanation point.

The prayer verse above sounds more like the words that Isaiah prayed (Isaiah 6:8). The Lord called Isaiah saying, *"Whom shall I send? Who will go for us?"* Isaiah's uncomplicated response was, *"Here I am ... send me!"* Note the explanation point.

The obvious point to be made here is that God sends whoever he "elects" to send. Both Moses (reluctantly) and Isaiah (a volunteer) were sent. This is another one of those verses you really need to think about before you pray. Do you really want to be sent?

Exodus 4:13 - Yet he [Moses] insisted, "If you please, Lord, send someone else!"

E1	The Lord is my banner.

What is the Lord to you? If you are like most people, you probably responded with answers like: "my savior", "my redeemer", "my friend, or "what?" You probably don't often respond, "The Lord is my banner."

In the inspirational verse below, we read that Moses built an altar, which he called "Yahweh-nissi," which means, "the LORD is my banner."[18]

What is a banner? There are several meanings for this noun, including:
1.) a sign bearing a motto, slogan, etc.,
2.) a long strip of cloth with a greeting, etc. lettered on it, and
3.) something attached to a staff as a battle standard.
In the inspirational verse below, Moses is apparently referring to the latter definition – a banner to raise in future military battles with Amalek.

Banners, as defined above, are all similar in that the person displaying the banner wants others to see it, the slogan, the greeting, or the battle standard. Banners are not made to hide. They are meant to be waved and displayed. Is the Lord your banner in times of battle? Do you proudly wave your banner?

Exodus 17:15-16: Moses also built an altar there [at Rephidim], which he called Yahweh-nissi; for he said, "The LORD takes in hand his banner; the LORD will war against Amalek through the centuries."

E2	My strength and my courage is the Lord. He has been my savior. He is my God and I praise him.

Wouldn't this be a great motto or slogan to print on your banner? The words in the prayer verse are almost a direct quote from the song that the Israelites sang to the Lord.

Exodus 15:1-3: Then Moses and the Israelites sang this song to the LORD: I will sing to the LORD, for he is gloriously triumphant; horse and chariot he has cast into the sea. **My strength and my courage is the LORD**, and **he has been my savior. He is my God, I praise him**; the God of my father, I extol him. The LORD is a warrior, LORD is his name!

E3	The Lord shall reign forever and ever.

The last section of the prayer (E1 - E3) voices adoration and praise for the Lord. Can you imagine the sound of every creature praying this verse?

*Then I heard every creature in heaven and on earth and under the earth
and in the sea, everything in the universe, cry out: "To the one who sits
on the throne and to the Lamb be blessing and honor, glory and might,
forever and ever." – Revelation 5:13*

Exodus 15:18 - The LORD shall reign forever and ever.

Why was the Pharaoh Obstinate?

As you read about the Egyptian plagues, you might ask the following questions:
- Why did the Lord make the Pharaoh obstinate?
- Why did the Pharaoh become hardhearted (again and again)?
- Did God make the Pharaoh sin?

The last question especially troubles me from time to time. What was the role of the Pharaoh (and Judas, and Pontius Pilate) in salvation history? Did the director of the play make the Pharaoh (and the others) stick to the script?

Look at the three verses from Exodus that I have included below. They give three different perspectives of what was happening during the time of the plagues. The first verse gives the impression that God was in charge – that God, like the director of a play, was making the Pharaoh sin. The last verse implies that the Pharaoh exercised his free will and sinned. The middle verse indicates that the Pharaoh knew what he was doing.

Exodus Verses	Who did what?	Similar to Exodus Verses
7:3-4	**Yet I [the LORD] will make Pharaoh so obstinate** *that, despite the many signs and wonders that I will work in the land of Egypt, he will not listen to you. ...*	9:12, 10:1, 10:20, 10:27, 11:10, 14:4, 14:8, 14:17
9:27	*Then Pharaoh summoned Moses and Aaron and said to them,* **"I have sinned again! The LORD is just;** *it is I and my subjects who are at fault. ..."*	
9:34-35	**But Pharaoh ... sinned again:** **he with his servants became obdurate,** *and in his obstinacy he would not let the Israelites go, as the LORD had foretold through Moses.*	7:22, 8:11, 8:15, 8:28, 9:7, 13:15

The table above and the story of the plagues bring up questions regarding:
- mankind's obstinacy and "hardness of the heart,"
- free will as it relates to God's will, and
- God's mercy.

I should warn you now. In the following sections things are going to get a little heavy. We are going to review how doctrines develop. Take a deep breath. Slow down your reading a bit and savor the words – savor the thoughts.

God, Moses, and Mercy

> *But the LORD said to Moses and Aaron, "Because you were not faithful to me in showing forth my sanctity before the Israelites, **you shall not lead this community into the land I will give them**." – Nm 20:12*

It really isn't clear from Scripture why God chose (in Nm 20:12 above) to "punish" (my word) Moses and Aaron as he did. After spending forty years meandering through the desert, why wasn't Moses allowed to lead His people into the Promised Land? Why wasn't Moses rewarded for his perseverance? As I noted previously, the "fault" is not clearly delineated in the Bible.

Because of God's stated reasoning – "because you were not faithful to me in showing forth my sanctity before the Israelites" – some connect the punishment with the fact that Moses struck the rock "twice" with his staff before "water gushed out in abundance." Did Moses strike the rock twice "because he had not sufficient faith to work the miracle with the first blow" or was the sin of Moses and Aaron doubting God's **mercy** toward the ever-rebellious people?[19]

There is that word again, **mercy**, to whom does God extend his **mercy**? Why didn't God extend more **mercy** to Moses, give him a little more slack?

Maybe it is just me. Maybe I am the only one that wonders why God made the Pharaoh obstinate, obdurate, and hardhearted. Maybe I am the only one that wonders why Moses and Aaron were punished – for hitting a rock twice?

Actually, it is reassuring to recognize that I am not the only one with these questions. They occurred first to St. Paul and later to St. Augustine. As Saints Paul and Augustine wrestled with these questions they developed Catholic doctrine – the doctrine that is incorporated into the *Catechism of the Catholic Church*.

We will take up those topics in the remainder of this chapter. You will find as you *pray Scripture* that you will – from time to time – take these little detours, as you try to better understand the Scripture that you are praying. Enjoy the detours. They are part of the process.

Hesed

The Hebrew word *hesed*, as used in the book of Exodus, is translated as **mercy** in most English Bibles. Most biblical scholars, however, agree that there is no single English word which is an adequate translation of what the Hebrews meant when they said and wrote *hesed*. And like most words, its meaning developed over the centuries.

To understand the rich meaning of a word like *hesed*, it is useful to study the words with which it is associated – the words that it was often paired with or used with. Biblical scholars have found that *hesed* was often associated with the Hebrew words that we translate as: steadfastness, loyalty, judgment, justice, righteousness, salvation, and peace.

As regards *hesed* and its use in the book of Exodus, four points are worth noting:

1. "This survey of some of the uses of the word illustrate why a single word [such as mercy] cannot translate its richness of meaning. ... The word [*hesed*] indicates a broad and embracing benevolence, a will to do good to another rather than evil. It is not precisely love or kindness but the goodness of the heart from which love and kindness arise."[20]

2. A basic meaning of the term *hesed*, which has not substantially changed over the centuries, is associated with the quality which makes another person worthy of faith.

3. The person who does *hesed* – the person who is merciful – is always in a superior position. God can be merciful to you. You cannot be merciful to God. The master can be merciful to his slave(s). The slave is not normally in a position to be merciful to his master.

4. Just as we struggle with the meaning of *hesed* and mercy; St. Paul struggled with the meanings of *hesed* and *eleos*[21] (the common Greek word used in the Septuagint translation); and St. Augustine struggled with the meanings of *hesed* and *misericordia* (the Latin word used in the Vulgate).

As you review the four points noted above, remember that just as it takes two to tango, it takes two for *hesed* to occur. It requires: (1) a quality which makes a person worthy of faith, and (2) a person (or God) in a superior position who has a broad and embracing benevolence. Consider these points as you read Saint Paul's and St. Augustine's comments on the Pharaoh, Moses, and "mercy."

Saint Paul's View

St. Paul, in his letter to the Romans, provided some input on the questions raised in Exodus:

> What then are we to say? Is there injustice on the part of God?
>
> Of course not! For he says to Moses: "I will show **mercy** to whom I will, I will take pity on whom I will." So it depends not upon a person's will or exertion, but upon God, who shows **mercy**.
>
> For the scripture says to Pharaoh,
>
> "This is why I have raised you up, to show my **power** through you that my name may be proclaimed throughout the earth."
>
> Consequently, **he has mercy upon whom he wills**, and he hardens whom he wills. – Romans 9:14-18

From the perspective of the risen Lord, "the gift of faith is the enactment of God's mercy [Romans 9:16]. God raised up Moses to display that mercy, and Pharaoh to display divine severity in punishing those who obstinately oppose their Creator."[22]

As regards the Pharaoh the basic biblical principle is: "those who will not see or hear *shall* not see or hear. On the other hand, the same God who thus makes stubborn or hardens the heart can reconstruct it through the work of the holy Spirit."[23]

St. Paul then goes on to ask:

> You will say to me then, "Why (then) does he still find fault? For who can oppose his will?" But who indeed are you, a human being, to talk back to God? Will what is made say to its maker, "Why have you created me so?" Or does not the potter have a right over the clay, to make out of the same lump one vessel for a noble purpose and another for an ignoble one?
>
> What if God, wishing to show his wrath and make known his power, has endured with **much patience** the vessels of wrath made for destruction? – Romans 9:19-22

St. Paul's response above "is less an explanation of God's ways than the rejection of an argument that places humanity on a level with God. At the same time, Paul shows that God is far less arbitrary than appearances suggest, for God endures **with much patience** a person like the Pharaoh of the Exodus."[24]

Saint Augustine's View

I don't often refer to the writing of the Fathers of the Church, those individuals such as St. Thomas Aquinas and St. Augustine that, with the help of the Holy Spirit, in turn helped the Church understand itself.

In this case, however, I will begin with some thoughts from St. Augustine, the then Bishop of Hippo, as recorded in *On Grace and Free Will*, which was written around 426 AD.

Before getting into his writings, let us marvel at the structure of the Church built by Christ on the rock of Peter. More than one thousand years before Columbus discovered the Americas, the Church was in place, the pope was St. Celestine I, and St. Augustine was the Bishop of Hippo. These two saints of the Church were also said to be friends and they communicated with each other on Church matters.[25]

Listed below are some thoughts by St. Augustine on the hearts of men, including the Pharaoh's hardened heart.[26]

> *God works in the hearts of men to incline their wills wherever He wills, whether to good deeds according to His **mercy**, or to evil after their own deserts; His own judgment being sometimes manifest, sometimes secret, but **always righteous**. …*
>
> *Therefore, whenever you read in the [Bible], that men are led aside, or that their hearts are blunted and hardened by God, never doubt that some ill deserts of their own have first occurred, so that they justly suffer these things. …*
>
> *Nor should you take away from Pharaoh **free will**, because in several passages God says, "I have hardened Pharaoh;" … for it does not by any means follow that Pharaoh did not, on this account, harden his own heart.*

Augustine continued to write on the above topic in Chapter 45 of the previously referenced treatise:

> *Be then well assured that your labour will never be in vain, if, setting before you a good purpose, you persevere in it to the last.*
>
> *For God, who fails to render, according to their deeds, only to those who He liberates, will then recompense every man according to His works.*
>
> *God will, therefore, certainly recompense both evil for evil, because He is just; and good for evil, because He is good; and good for good, because He is good and just. Only, evil for good He will never recompense, because He is not unjust.*

He will, therefore, recompense evil for evil – punishment for unrighteousness;
and He will recompense good for evil – grace for unrighteousness;
and He will recompense good for good – grace for grace.

Mercy: Paraphrasing St. Paul and St. Augustine

- God rewards the good because God is good and just (grace for grace).
- God punishes the evil because God is just.
- God will show mercy to whoever God wants to (grace for unrighteousness).
- God will never punish the good because God is just.

So what do you think? Are the four statements above fair? Is God fair to man? Was God fair to the Pharaoh? Was God fair to Moses?

The four statements seem fair to me. God recompenses good for good – grace for grace. Our labor will never be in vain – if we preserve to the last.

From a theological perspective, Exodus clearly shows us who really is "God." From that perspective and in a manner consistent with the insight provided by Saints Paul and Augustine:

- **The Pharaoh was evil (a false God).**
- God punishes the Pharaoh because the Pharaoh is evil and God is just.
- God did not choose to show the Pharaoh any mercy.
- God is in charge and Exodus is written to stress this fact.
- God uses the Pharaoh (evil) to demonstrate how evil is punished.
- God received glory through the Pharaoh (Exodus 14:17, Prayer Verse A2).

God apparently chose to show us, via the Pharaoh, how severely he is prepared to treat those who are obstinate, obdurate, and incredulous towards him.

Question: Could God have chosen to show an obstinate, obdurate, and incredulous person mercy?

Answer: "There are no limits to the mercy of God, but anyone who deliberately refuses to accept his mercy by repenting, rejects the forgiveness of his sins and the salvation offered by the Holy Spirit. Such hardness of heart can lead to final impenitence and eternal loss" (CCC 1864). "By going so far as to give up his own Son for us, God reveals that he is 'rich in mercy'" (CCC 211).

Moses and Mercy

My previous question regarding why Moses was punished – why he was not allowed to enter the Promised Land before he died – is a little more difficult for me to understand.

> *Stop judging, that you may not be judged. – Mt 7:1*

The verse above, from Matthew, reminds me that it is not my "job" to try to figure it out. It is not my job to try to understand, approve, or disapprove what God does.

> *… I will pronounce my name, "LORD"; I who show favors to whom I will, I who grant **mercy** to whom I will. – Ex 33:19*
>
> *For he says to Moses: "I will show **mercy** to whom I will, I will take pity on whom I will." – Rom 9:15*

The verses above – first the Lord's answer to Moses in Exodus and then Saint Paul's reiteration of that answer – remind me that it is not my job to determine who deserves God's mercy, to approve God's decision or to question it. God grants mercy to whom he wants to.

> *Nor does the Father judge anyone, but he has given all judgment to his Son, … – John 5:22*

The verse above reminds me that all judgment has now been given to Jesus. It is comforting for me to remember that, from the perspective of the risen Lord, the gift of faith – to me and to you – is the enactment of God's mercy.

Lastly, I am reminded that while Moses was not allowed to enter the Promised Land before he died, he was seen in the Promised Land, on the top of the mountain with Jesus at a later time (Mt 17:3-4, Mk 9:4-5). God grants mercy to whom he wants, when he wants, and in the manner that he wants.

Free Will

The preceding sections provided some insight on how Catholic doctrines develop. They begin with Scripture, such as St. Paul's letter to the Romans. Over time that Scripture and "Tradition" are developed by the magisterium with input from the "Apostolic Fathers" and the "Doctors of the Church," such as St. Augustine (the Doctor of grace). This developed doctrine, from time to time, is summarized and incorporated into catechisms for wider dissemination and teaching.[27]

The doctrines associated with "free will" have always interested me. God could have made us (i.e., our nature) obeying and unthinking slaves or robots. Instead, he chose to let us determine our response to his love. We humans are given the freedom to determine how we choose to love, honor, and obey our creator and savior – to the extent that we believe that he is our creator and savior. Or we can choose to be obstinate, obdurate, or hardhearted.

Listed below are a few citations from the *Catechism of the Catholic Church*, regarding this topic. Think about how they relate to the Pharaoh, the story of the plagues, and your life.

> *God created man a rational being, conferring on him the dignity of a person who can initiate and control his own actions. … Man is rational and therefore like God;* **he is created with free will and is master over his acts***. – CCC 1730*

> *Freedom is the power, rooted in reason and will, to act or not to act, to do this or that, and so to perform deliberate actions on one's own responsibility. By* **free will** *one shapes one's own life. – CCC 1731*

> *The choice to disobey and do evil is an abuse of freedom and leads to "***the slavery of sin.***" – CCC 1733*

> *The root of sin is in the heart of man, in his* **free will***, according to the teaching of the Lord: .... – CCC 1853*

> ***God is in no way, directly or indirectly, the cause of moral evil.*** *He permits it, however, because he respects the freedom of his creatures and, mysteriously, knows how to derive good from it: ….* *– CCC 311*

As I reread the citations from the *Catechism* above, it was almost like rereading the story of the plagues in Exodus. The Pharaoh (not a god) was created with free will and was responsible for his actions. The Hebrews were trying to escape slavery and the Pharaoh was a slave to sin. The root of sin is in the heart of man and the Pharaoh had a hard heart.

Dispositions of the Heart

I have noted the many references in the first eighteen chapters of Exodus to the Pharaoh's hardened heart. **In a biblical sense, what is the condition of your heart?** Consider these citations from the *Catechism*:

> But this search for God demands of man every effort of intellect, a sound will, *"an upright heart,"* as well as the witness of others who teach him to seek God. – CCC 30

> The spiritual tradition of the Church also emphasizes the **heart**, in the biblical sense of the depths of one's being, where the person decides for or against God. – CCC 368

> The Holy Spirit gives a spiritual understanding of the Word of God to those who read or hear it, according to the dispositions of their **hearts**. – CCC 1101

> The Holy Spirit prepares the faithful for **the sacraments** by the Word of God and the faith which welcomes that word in **well-disposed hearts**. Thus the sacraments **strengthen faith and express it.** – CCC 1133

> Through his Word, God speaks to man. By words, mental or vocal, our prayer takes flesh. Yet it is most important that the **heart** should be present to him to whom we are speaking in prayer: "Whether or not our prayer is heard depends not on the number of words, but on the fervor of our souls." – CCC 2700.

Note again the words above (from CCC 1133) that the sacraments – the topic of Volume 2 in this series – "strengthen faith and express it."

Catechism Check?

I believe that the prayer in this chapter is consistent with the *Catechism of the Catholic Church*.

Most of the *Catechism* references used were found via the online *Catechism* and the search feature therein. I queried words such as obstinate, obdurate, forever, hardhearted, and heart.

We Can Pray!

Is the Lord your banner?

Are you sometimes obstinate, obdurate, or incredulous?

Does God show you mercy?

Why does God choose to show mercy to some – but not others?

Does it matter?

Our challenge in life is to determine God's will and then to decide (our choice) to act accordingly. Free will is God's blessing to us. We are not puppets. We control our destinies. The challenge is not impossible, but it does require God's grace.

Jesus aimed us in the right direction when he taught us how to pray. He told us to ask the Father to deliver us from the evil one's temptation so that we can die the death of the just. Our challenge is to avoid temptation, to distance ourselves from the evil one.

Can we align our free will with God's will?

We can pray! I suggest that we start with *The Lord's Prayer.* Pray it often and pray it with passion.

> *Our Father, who art in heaven, hallowed be thy name.*
> *Thy kingdom come, thy will be done on earth as it is*
> *in heaven. Give us this day our daily bread; and forgive*
> *us our trespasses, as we forgive those who trespass*
> *against us; and **lead us not into temptation**, but*
> *deliver us from evil. Amen.*

We can remember: From the perspective of the risen Lord, the gift of faith – to me and to you – is the enactment of God's mercy.

Chapter 3

"The Ark" Prayer

Prayer	Vs.	Inspiration
Lord, fill me with your glory, as you filled the Dwelling containing the ark,	A1	Ex 40:34
the ark where your commandments were placed.	A2	Ex 25:16
Have your angels spread their wings over me, as they were stretched out above the ark,	B1	Ex 25:20
the ark where your commandments were placed.	B2	Ex 25:21
I pray that my faith is as strong as the poles that carried the ark, the poles that were to remain forever with the ark,	C1	Ex 25:13-15
the ark where your commandments were put.	C2	Ex 40:3
I pray that my soul is as pure as the gold that covered the ark,	D1	Ex 25:11
the ark that contained the jar of manna, the ark that contained Aaron's staff, the ark that contained the tablets of the covenant.	D2	Heb 9:3-4
I pray that I meet you there, in that intimate space between the angels on the ark, in that space from which you told Moses your commands.	E1	Ex 25:22

Background

"The Ark" Prayer was the second prayer that I wrote. Two weeks after I wrote my first prayer, as described in the previous chapter, my Bible study's "optional challenge" read: "Do a sketch, painting, or model of the Ark, the tent, of some object within them, or write a poem or prayer inspired by the Ark."[28]

I again reviewed the gifts that God had given me. Since they had not changed, I quickly ruled out (in order) the painting, the sketch, the model, and the poem. All that was left was "prayer inspired by the ark."

A little Old Testament review might be appropriate before I move on. The **ark of the covenant** was initially built by the Hebrews to hold and preserve the tablets that the Ten Commandments were written on, as they journeyed through the desert on their way to the Promised Land.

From a practical perspective, the ark was a small portable box or chest, roughly the size of a child's coffin, made from wood. Because of its contents, however, it was built to high standards, and it was very ornate (e.g., overlaid with gold inside and out, two Cherubim (angels) on top), as described in Exodus 25.

The ark led the Hebrews as they traveled through the desert. Two special poles, overlaid with gold, were attached to the ark through rings on both sides. These poles were used by the priests to support and carry the ark.

I found a beautiful painting of the ark on the internet.[29] The painting depicted how one artist envisioned the ark. The poles used to carry the ark were in place, as specified. The gold ark glistened in front of a black background. The wings of the Cherubim swept up from both ends and almost touched above the center of the ark and between the wings of the Cherubim there was a bright light, like the sun starting to peak above the horizon.

The painting provided me with some additional inspiration. It was an example of the religious art that taught my Catholic ancestors – when Scripture was not as readily available. As Graham noted: "They were taught through paintings and statuary and frescos in the churches, which portrayed before their eyes the doctrines of the faith and truths of Scripture ...".[30]

The prayer that I wrote was relatively brief. I typed it out, printed it along with the picture, attached it to the rest of that week's homework and turned it in. When Deb, the study leader, returned the homework the following week, she had written the following note below the prayer:

*"You **pray the Scripture** well. I trust that you experience God's answers as well. Thank you for sharing this heartfelt prayer."*

There were those words again "**pray the Scripture**." The assignment was to write a prayer but somehow, I was praying Scripture. The prayers I wrote were reflecting Scripture. They were my words but, in many ways, I was more of an editor than an author. The prayers were, for the most part, God's words as written in Scripture.

Since six of the lines from the prayer begin with, "the ark," I chose those words for the title of the prayer. Sometimes, I wish that I had more imagination.

The prayer is about "the ark" but we must remember that this was no ordinary little wooden chest. It led the Hebrews through the desert. It circled Jericho (Joshua 6) for seven consecutive days, before the walls of that city collapsed. From a Catholic perspective, it prefigured the Church, and it prefigures Mary, the mother of God (as I will describe later in this chapter).

"The Ark" Prayer - How is it Structured?

Let's take a look at this prayer. How is it structured? What are some of the key components of the prayer?

Overview

As I noted, this was the second prayer that I wrote, and I wrote it some time ago. I didn't realize it at the time, but the prayer is almost entirely a prayer of petition. There is a little bit of thankful adoration and praise mixed into some of the verses, but it is, by and large, a prayer of petition.

This prayer and the associated inspirational verses are intentionally repetitive. You will note that prayer verses A2, B2, C2 and D2 are similar in that they all refer to what was contained in the ark. After all, what is contained in the ark is what is most important. As you study Scripture, you will note that at times Scripture is repetitive. Scripture sometimes contains:

- the same or similar stories,

- instructions on how to do something – followed by details on how that something was done, or

- the same details repeated for no apparent reason other than maybe bad editing.

Scripture scholars tell us that some items were repeated because they were very important. A modern-day teaching tip is to:

(1) tell them what you are going to tell them,

(2) tell them, and then

(3) tell them what you told them.

This teaching tip, like the Old Testament writing style, uses repetition to make sure that the students (e.g., the chosen people) get the message.

This prayer is also a little broader in scope than the previous prayer. My first prayer (Chapter 2) was (by instruction) confined to the first eighteen chapters of Exodus. This prayer is intended to describe "the ark," and Scripture speaks of the ark in other Old and New Testament books. One of the prayer verses, as such, was inspired by a verse in Hebrews.

I will now go through the prayer "verse-by verse," and then I will write a little about the theology of "the four senses of Scripture" and something called *typology*.

Verse by Verse

A1	**Lord, fill me with your glory,** **as you filled the Dwelling containing the ark,**
	A cloud covered the meeting tent, and the glory of the Lord filled the dwelling. The prayer begins with a bit of adoration (e.g., "your glory") and a petition. The petition asks that the Holy Spirit (i.e., the cloud) fill me, as it filled the dwelling place of the Lord on earth. "*Cloud and light.* These two images occur together in the manifestations of the Holy Spirit. In the theophanies of the Old Testament, the cloud, now obscure, now luminous, reveals the living and saving God, while veiling the transcendence of his glory ..." (CCC 697).
	Exodus 40:34 - Then the cloud covered the meeting tent, and the glory of the LORD filled the Dwelling.

A2	the ark where your commandments were placed.

As I previously noted, the Hebrews built the ark for the specific purpose of storing and preserving the tablets containing the "Ten Commandments," as the people of God journeyed through the desert.

A more formal name for the Ten Commandments is "Decalogue," which means literally "ten words." God revealed these "ten words" to his people on the holy mountain. They were written "with the finger of God" (cf. CCC 2056).

> *Moses then turned and came down the mountain with the two tablets of the commandments in his hands, tablets that were written on both sides, front and back; tablets that were made by God, having inscriptions on them that were engraved by God himself. – Ex 32:15-16*

Moses broke the above-mentioned tablets shortly thereafter in a fit of anger. When he came down from the mountain, he saw the chosen people of God sinning. He found them worshipping a false God (the golden calf). God, in his mercy, later engraved a second set of tablets. Because of God's mercy, they were even more precious. They needed to be preserved. They would be safely stored in the ark of the covenant as the Hebrews continued their journey through the desert.

Exodus 25:16 - In the ark you are to put the commandments which I will give you.

B1	Have your angels spread their wings over me, as they were stretched out above the ark,

The second section of the prayer is also a petition. The design of the ark called for two cherubim (angels) to be placed, like statues, on the top of the ark. The design was very specific as to their placement and their wings were to be "stretched out," to protect the ark below. The outstretched angel wings remind me of the outstretched wings of a mother bird, protecting one of her brood that has fallen to the ground.

The Church (CCC 336) reassures me: "From infancy to death human life is surrounded by their watchful care and intercession. 'Beside each believer stands an angel as protector and shepherd leading him to life.' Already here on earth the Christian life shares by faith in the blessed company of angels and men united in God."

The Church, via the "Cherubic Hymn" of the Byzantine Liturgy celebrates the memory of certain angels, including our guardian angels (cf. CCC 335).

Exodus 25:20 - The cherubim shall have their wings spread out above, covering the propitiatory with them; they shall be turned toward each other, but with their faces looking toward the propitiatory.

B2	the ark where your commandments were placed.

The repetition begins. Just five verses earlier (Exodus 25:16, prayer verse A2), similar words were used. **God's commandments are important.** They are our part of the covenant. We should take care not to lose them, forget them, or worse yet, break them. By repeating this phrase, this prayer acknowledges the importance of the commandments.

> *"Here, then," said the LORD, "is the covenant I will make. Before the eyes of all your people I will work such marvels as have never been wrought in any nation anywhere on earth, so that this people among whom you live may see how awe-inspiring are the deeds which I, the LORD, will do at your side. **But you, on your part**, **must keep the commandments** I am giving you today. … – Exodus 34:10-11*

Exodus 25:21 - This propitiatory you shall then place on top of the ark. In the ark itself you are to put the commandments which I will give you.

C1	I pray that my faith is as strong as the poles that carried the ark, the poles that were to remain forever with the ark,

This petition continues in this section of the prayer. Two poles were constructed to assist the priests carry the ark as the chosen people journeyed through the desert. The ark, with all its wood and the gold overlay, was heavy. The poles served as handles, and they helped distribute the load. The poles had to be both strong and flexible, as the Church must be and is.

Later in this chapter, I write about the death of Uzzah, as it relates to the ark of the covenant and the poles designed to carry it.

Exodus 25:13-15: Then make poles of acacia wood and plate them with gold. These poles you are to put through the rings on the sides of the ark, for carrying it; they must remain in the rings of the ark and never be withdrawn.

C2	the ark where your commandments were put.

The repetition continues. God's commandments are important.

Exodus 40:3 - Put the ark of the commandments in it, and screen off the ark with the veil.

D1	I pray that my soul is as pure as the gold that covered the ark,

Many artisans were needed to construct the ark, including designers, carpenters, woodcarvers, sculptors (for the cherubim), metalsmiths, and metallurgists. The gold was to be **pure**. A skilled metallurgist would be required to refine the gold. It was to be as **pure** as humanly possible. The prayer's petition to God is that my soul be as pure as the gold that covered the ark – as **pure** as humanly possible.

"Since God could create everything out of nothing, he can also, through the Holy Spirit, give spiritual life to sinners by creating a **pure** heart in them" ... (CCC 298).

"'**Pure** in heart' refers to those who have attuned their intellects and wills to the demands of God's holiness, chiefly in three areas: charity; chastity or sexual rectitude; love of truth and orthodoxy of faith" (CCC 2518).

"The '**pure** in heart' are promised that they will see God face to face and be like him. Purity of heart is the precondition of the vision of God. Even now It enables us to see *according* to God, to accept others as 'neighbors'; it lets us perceive the human body ... as a temple of the Holy Spirit" ... (CCC 2519).

Exodus 25:11 - Plate it inside and outside with **pure** gold, and put a molding of gold around the top of it.

D2	the ark that contained the jar of manna, the ark that contained Aaron's staff, the ark that contained the tablets of the covenant.

The repetition continues. God's commandments are important.

But wait, something is different, something is new. The prayer switches from Exodus to the New Testament letter to the Hebrews and now, in addition to the commandments, there is news that the ark of the covenant contains more than just the covenant.

It appears that sometime after the days of exodus, after a permanent temple was built, some additional important things were placed in the ark of the covenant: a jar of manna and Aaron's staff. What did this mean at the time and what does it mean to me today?

In the "Mary - a Type of Ark" section of this chapter, I will return to the contents of the ark described above.

Hebrews 9:3-4: Behind the second veil was the tabernacle called the Holy of Holies, in which were the gold altar of incense and the ark of the covenant entirely covered with gold. In it were the gold jar containing the manna, the staff of Aaron that had sprouted, and the tablets of the covenant.

E1	I pray that I meet you there, in that intimate space between the angels on the ark, in that space from which you told Moses your commands.

The prayer ends with a huge petition.

The imagery of this prayer verse and the inspirational words of the Lord are magnificent.

In the inspirational verse below, the Lord asks Moses to meet him above the ark, between the two cherubim. How big is this space? Why meet there? Is this heaven?

From the descriptions that we have of the ark of the covenant, the space between the tips of the cherubim's wings is miniscule. From a human perspective, a meeting with God there would indeed be intimate. Can heaven be this small or is it as vast as we usually picture it? How can a space so small be so vast?

The prayer verse elicits a lot of questions. Just as the prayer verse imagery and the imagery of the Exodus 25:22 are magnificent, so are the teachings of the Church.

"This biblical expression [who art in heaven] does not mean a place ('space'), but a way of being; it does not mean that God is distant, but majestic" (CCC 2794).

"'Our Father who art in heaven' is rightly understood to mean that God is in the hearts of the just, as in his holy temple. At the same time, it means that those who pray should desire the one they invoke to dwell in them."[31]

"The symbol of the heavens refers us back to the mystery of the covenant we are living when we pray to our Father. He is in heaven, his dwelling place; the Father's house is our homeland" (CCC 2795).

Exodus 25:22 - There I will meet you and there, from above the propitiatory, between the two cherubim on the ark of the commandments, I will tell you all the commands that I wish you to give the Israelites.

The Ark and Uzzah

As was noted in prayer verse C1, poles were designed to carry the ark as the Hebrews journeyed through the desert. Centuries later, as documented in 2 Samuel 6 and 1 Chronicles 13, King David was also transporting the ark. At that time, however, he decided to change the mode of transportation from "priests and poles" to a less burdensome "ark on cart" method, with oxen doing most of the work. Both biblical accounts are printed below. They are similar but not the same. I suggest that you concentrate on the **bold** version of what happened.

Vs.	2 Samuel 6	Vs.	1 Chronicles 13
3-4	**The ark of God was placed on a new cart and taken away from the house of Abinadab on the hill. Uzzah and Ahio, sons of Abinadab, guided the cart, with Ahio walking before it,**	7	They transported the ark of God on a new cart from the house of Abinadab; Uzzah and Ahio were guiding the cart,
5	**while David and all the Israelites made merry before the LORD with all their strength, with singing and with citharas, harps, tambourines, sistrums and cymbals.**	8	while David and all Israel danced before God with great enthusiasm, amid songs and music on lyres, harps, tambourines, cymbals, and trumpets.
6	**When they came to the threshing floor of Nodan, Uzzah reached out his hand to the ark of God and steadied it, for the oxen were making it tip.**	9	As they reached the threshing floor of Chidon, Uzzah stretched out his hand to steady the ark, for the oxen were upsetting it.
7	But the LORD was angry with Uzzah; God struck him on that spot, and he died there before God.	10	**Then the LORD became angry with Uzzah and struck him; he died there in God's presence, because he had laid his hand on the ark.**
8	David was disturbed because the LORD had vented his anger on Uzzah. (The place has been called Perez-uzzah down to the present day.)	11	**David was disturbed because the LORD'S anger had broken out against Uzzah. Therefore that place has been called Perez-uzza even to this day.**
9	David feared the LORD that day and said, "How can the ark of the LORD come to me?"	12	**David was now afraid of God, and he said, "How can I bring the ark of God with me?"**
10	So David would not have the ark of the LORD brought to him in the City of David, but diverted it to the house of Obededom the Gittite.	13	**Therefore he did not take the ark back with him to the City of David, but he took it instead to the house of Obededom the Gittite.**

The Ark and Uzzah (continued)

Wow – what happened? Let me see if I read these accounts correctly. As the "cart with the ark" was rolling down the road, King David and all Israel danced with all their strength. But then, in a fraction of a second, a very disturbing thing happened to the cart – "oxen were making it tip." Uzzah, one of the men who was walking along side of the cart, reached out to steady the ark and as he did so he touched it. Then the Lord became angry with Uzzah and struck him; he died there *in God's presence*, because he had laid his hand on the ark. David then became disturbed because of the Lord's anger, became afraid of God, and decided not to take the ark back to the city of David.

Wow – what happened? King David took a short cut – allowed an ox drawn cart to transport the ark – and danced along the route. The oxen decided to make the cart tip; Uzzah was killed by God because he touched the ark; and King David became afraid of God.

Have you ever taken a short cut and had things go bad? If so, you can probably appreciate King David's situation.

I have no great insight as to what happened on that day or its impact on salvation history. Traditionally, Uzzah's death has been an example of what happens when one does not have the proper fear of, or respect for, the Lord. That is, most likely, what the deuteronomic historians were trying to stress when they wrote the passages in 2 Samuel.

Uzzah's death and the Lord's anger are troublesome to many. This story even drives some people away from God. They see a mean-spirited God. The punishment, to our human eyes, certainly does not appear to be consistent with the crime (reacting instinctively, keeping the ark upright – as the cart apparently did not tip). But then again you and I are not God, as we so often forget.

Maybe this was God's way to get David's attention. Maybe David needed to be more afraid of God – to be more reverent. Maybe this was not the time to dance. Maybe the Lord was angry because he had to kill Uzzah because of the shortcut that David took.

The Ark and Uzzah (continued)

One thought comes to mind, however, when I read these accounts and that is how we Christians so quickly associate death with "bad" and how readily we dispatch (in our minds) so many of God's children to hell when they die.

Scripture (1 Chronicles 13:10) tells us that:
A. The Lord became angry with Uzzah and struck him; and
B. Uzzah died there *in God's presence* because he had laid his hand on the ark.

Logic would tell us that there is a strong connection between A and B but maybe the connection is a little weaker than we first suspected.

A few paragraphs back, I suggested a few reasons why God might have been angry with Uzzah and David. Now let me suggest one other reason why Uzzah died. Could it be that when he touched the ark, he experienced God – that when he touched the ark he was *in God's presence*? Could it be that he no longer needed to live? Could it be that Uzzah died a martyr's death by saving the ark?

Where is Uzzah today – heaven, hell, purgatory or somewhere else? Only God knows for sure. Look to your answer, and your confidence in it, to tell you something about your theological and spiritual relationship with God.

Scripture does not tell us how old Uzzah was. He apparently was healthy enough to walk along the cart and prevent it from tipping. He may have been struck down in the prime of life. Is it better to die at age 30 or 80? Let me rephrase the question; is it better to die at age 30 and go to heaven, or to die at 80 and go to hell?

Uzzah was on a journey when he died. We too are on a journey. We journey on this earth until we die and, unfortunately, we are not always in good standing with God as we journey along.

Most people consider Uzzah to be a "bit player" in salvation history. King David was the "biblical biggie" in 2 Samuel 6 and 1 Chronicles 13. We must continue to remind ourselves that we all have a role in salvation history. We must all try to keep the ark (the Church?) upright, so that we to can someday be *in God's presence*.

"God has bound salvation to the sacrament of Baptism, but he himself is not bound by his sacraments."[32]

The Four Senses of Scripture (cf. CCC 115 - 118)

Before getting further into *praying Scripture* and the remainder of prayers in this book, I feel the need to step back and discuss two aspects of how the Church views Scripture. The first aspect involves what are referred to as "the four senses of Scripture." Unlike some of our Christian brethren, who limit themselves to, or at least focus on the "literal sense" of Scripture, the Church appreciates Scripture via all four of the senses listed below:

Literal sense – the literal meaning conveyed by the words of Scripture. The "literal" speaks of **deeds**.

Allegorical sense – the significance of an event "in Christ." The "allegory" speaks of **faith through Christ**.

Moral sense – the significance of an event should prompt us to "act justly." The "moral" sense teaches us **how to act**.

Anagogical sense – the "eternal" significance of an event. "Anagogy" is **our destiny**. The Church on earth is a sign of the heavenly Jerusalem.[33]

Examples - The Four Senses of Scripture

Some examples may help demonstrate the four senses of Scripture. All the examples can be viewed according to the four senses described above. This is not true of all verses; most verses only have a literal meaning. The last example concerns the ark of the covenant.[34]

Example 1 (1 Kings 19:5-8):

> *[Elijah] lay down and fell asleep under the broom tree, but then an angel touched him and ordered him to get up and eat. He looked and there at his head was a hearth cake and a jug of water. After he ate and drank, he lay down again, but the angel of the LORD came back a second time, touched him, and ordered, "Get up and eat, else the journey will be too long for you!" He got up, ate and drank; then strengthened by that food, he walked forty days and forty nights to the mountain of God, Horeb.*

- Literal   The passage describes Elijah's journey to Mt. Horeb.
- Allegorical   Jesus' 40 day fast and the Eucharist (Matthew 4:1-4)
- Moral   The passage calls us to partake of the Eucharist.
- Anagogical   Longing for the bread of life, we journey to heaven.

Example 2 (Psalm 84:2-3):

How lovely your dwelling, O LORD of hosts! My soul yearns and pines for the courts of the LORD. My heart and flesh cry out for the living God.

- Literal   The verses speak of the Jerusalem temple.
- Allegorical   The verses speak of the Church that Christ founded.
- Moral   My inmost spirit is where God dwells.
- Anagogical   The verses speak of heaven.

Example 3 (Revelation 11:19 – 12:2):

*Then God's temple in heaven was opened, and the **ark of his covenant** could be seen in the temple. There were flashes of lightning, rumblings, and peals of thunder, an earthquake, and a violent hailstorm. A great sign appeared in the sky, **a woman** clothed with the sun, with the moon under her feet, and on her head a crown of twelve stars. She was with child and wailed aloud in pain as she labored to give birth.*

- Literal   The ark and a woman in labor were seen in heaven.
- Allegorical   The ark was Mary, the mother of Christ.
- Moral   We should honor Mary's spiritual motherhood.
- Anagogical   We can see God and Mary, his mother, in heaven.

Reread the example passages and look for the **deeds** and **faith** described. Look for the instructions and/or examples of **how to act** – examples of how life should be lived. And finally, look for how they foretell our collective **destiny**.

One of the great things about "the four senses" of Scripture is that they do not limit us to "a" meaning. There may be multiple meanings for man and his Church. The ark in the above passage may also have meaning to some as "Eve" or "the Church" herself.

Theology of Typology

The second and somewhat related aspect of how the Church views Scripture (in addition to "the four senses") is called **typology**. The *Catechism of Catholic Church* does an excellent job of describing typology, as can be witnessed below.

The mystery of Christ can be found under the letter of the Old Testament. It is called "**typological**" because the newness of Christ is revealed on the basis of the "figures" (**types**) which announce him in the deeds, words, and symbols of the first covenant, the covenant described in the Old Testament. These Old Testament deeds, words and symbols were unveiled first by Christ and then by the apostles and fathers of the Church (cf. CCC 1094).

Examples:

- "Thus the flood and Noah's ark prefigured salvation by Baptism, as did the cloud and the crossing of the Red Sea.

- Water from the rock was the figure of the spiritual gifts of Christ, and

- manna in the desert prefigured the Eucharist, 'the true bread from heaven'" (CCC 1094, bullets added).

"The Church, as early as apostolic times, and then constantly in her Tradition, has illuminated the unity of the divine plan in the two Testaments through **typology**, which discerns in God's works of the Old Covenant prefigurations of what he accomplished in the fullness of time in the person of his incarnate Son" (CCC 128).

"Christians therefore read the Old Testament in the light of Christ crucified and risen. Such **typological** reading discloses the inexhaustible content of the Old Testament; but it must not make us forget that the Old Testament retains its own intrinsic value as Revelation reaffirmed by our Lord himself. Besides, the New Testament has to be read in the light of the Old. Early Christian catechesis made constant use of the Old Testament. As an old saying put it, the New Testament lies hidden in the Old and the Old Testament is unveiled in the New" (CCC 129).

"**Typology** indicates the dynamic movement toward the fulfillment of the divine plan when 'God (will) be everything to everyone.' Nor do the calling of the patriarchs and the exodus from Egypt, for example, lose their own value in God's plan, from the mere fact that they were intermediate stages" (CCC 130).

Mary - a Type of Ark

Scott Hahn, in his book *Hail, Holy Queen: The Mother of God in the Word of God* does a masterful job equating the Mother of God to the ark of the covenant.[35]

In Chapter 3, *Venerators of the Lost Ark*, he notes that the Jews who first read the book of Revelation would have been jarred by the reference in verse 11:19 to the ark, which had been missing for six centuries. [Refer back to Example 3 in the previous section for the biblical text – Rev 11:19 - 12:2.]

Scott Hahn does an excellent job of stepping his readers through Scripture and providing us with the allegorical sense of Scripture. I encourage you to read his book to more fully appreciate the insight that he has regarding Mary. For my purposes, however, I will just highlight four quotes from Hahn's book:[36]

> *John has shown us the ark of the covenant – and it is a woman.*
>
> *What made the ark holy was that it contained the covenant.*
>
> *Whatever made the ark holy made Mary even holier. If the first ark contained the Word of God in stone, Mary's body contained the Word of God enfleshed. If the first ark contained miraculous bread from heaven, Mary's body contained the very Bread of Life that conquers death forever. If the first ark contained the rod of the long-ago ancestral priest, Mary's body contained the divine person of the eternal priest, Jesus Christ.*
>
> *John saw the ark of the new covenant, the vessel chosen to bear God's covenant into the world once and for all.*

Hail Mary full of grace, the Lord is with thee: The angel's greeting to Mary, which we cite when we say the *Ave Maria* (the *Hail Mary*), tells us that Mary is full of grace because the Lord is with her.

- The grace with which she is filled is the **presence of him** who is the source of all grace. Mary, in whom the Lord himself has just made his dwelling, is the daughter of Zion in person, the **ark of the covenant**, the place where the glory of the Lord dwells.

- **Full of grace**, Mary is wholly given over to him who has come to dwell in her and whom she is about to give to the world.

- "Mary, because of her faith, became **the mother of believers**, through whom all nations of the earth receive him who is God's own blessing: Jesus, the 'fruit of thy womb'" (CCC 2676).

Catechism Check?

I believe that the prayer in this chapter is consistent with the *Catechism of the Catholic Church*.

The comments on Uzzah in this chapter are mine. As best I can determine, neither the *Catechism* nor the Church address where the soul of Uzzah is today.

The "Four Senses of Scripture" examples were developed from other sources as noted. They may or may not reflect official Church teachings.

I utilized the search capability of the on-line *Catechism of the Catholic Church*[37] heavily for this chapter. I searched for words such as: ark, cloud, commandments, angel, cherubim, pure, heaven, types, and typology.

We Can Pray!

I think that this *"The Ark" Prayer* and this chapter provide some insight into what treasures can be found in Scripture when you look a little harder, with all your literary senses and some appreciation for typology.

The subtitle of this book infers that the subjects of the book are some biblical characters. Along the way, I have promised some "biblical biggies" – some scriptural "stars." So what have I delivered in this chapter: a prayer about a box and some thoughts about a man who carried it.

The ark was indeed a box, but if that is all that it is to you, you have missed a lot of the beauty in Scripture. You may even have missed some insights about Mary, the mother of God.

Is your faith as strong as the poles that carried the ark?

Is your soul as pure as the gold that covered the ark?

Will you meet the Lord in that intimate space between the angels on the ark?

We can pray – we can at least start with prayer!

Chapter 4

A Tribute to Joshua

A Tribute to Joshua	Vs.	Inspiration Verse Joshua
Lord, God, your hand is mighty.	A1	4:23-24
You commanded Joshua to be firm and steadfast, to avoid the right and to avoid the left, so that he would succeed wherever he went.	A2	1:7
He acted accordingly and left nothing undone.	A3	11:15
You halted the waters of the Jordan for him;	A4	3:15-16
You delivered Jericho and its king to his power;	A5	6.2
and his fame spread throughout the land.	A6	6:27
Joshua said to his people:	B1	24:22
• Serve the Lord completely and sincerely.	B2	24:14
• Do not be afraid or dismayed – be firm and steadfast instead.	B3	10:25
• Keep the law on your lips – so that you will attain your goal.	B4	1:8
• Take great care, however, to love the Lord, your God.	B5	23:11
The words of the law were read – both the blessings and the curses.	B6	8:34
Joshua's people listened and they chose to serve you.	B7	24:22
Lord, God of glory and honor:	C1	7:19
You did not leave or forsake Joshua.	C2	1:5
Every promise you made to him was fulfilled.	C3	23:14
Joshua prayed to you and the sun stood still.	C4	10:12-13
Never before or since was there a day like that, when the Lord obeyed the voice of a man.	C5	10:14
Lord, God of gods:	D1	22:22
You gave Israel all the land that you promised. You gave them peace on every side. You brought all their enemies under their power. None of your promises were broken – everyone was fulfilled.	D2	21:43-45

Background

My Bible study had finishing studying the Pentateuch, the first five books of the Old Testament. We had spent twenty weeks studying these important books, starting with Exodus (7 weeks) and ending with Genesis (7 weeks). The books of Leviticus, Numbers, and Deuteronomy were sandwiched in-between. The book of Joshua would start our third semester. The Pentateuch ended with the death and burial of Moses in Deuteronomy 34. In that last chapter in Deuteronomy (verse 9) we read:

> Now **Joshua**, son of Nun, was filled with the spirit of wisdom, since Moses had laid his hands upon him; and so the Israelites gave him their obedience, thus carrying out the LORD's command to Moses.

Salvation history was turned over to a man named **Joshua** and that history would be recorded in a book with the same name.

Joshua the Book

Joshua is for the most part an historical book – a "sacred" history as such.

The first six chapters recall two miraculous events: the crossing of the Jordan River and the capture of Jericho ("and the walls came tumbling down").

Chapters 7-12 describe other military campaigns that Joshua led throughout "the promised land" – through the foothills from Jericho; first to the west, then to the south, and finally to the north. **Joshua was a warrior for God**.

Chapters 13-21 are, for the most part, boring descriptions of the tribal boundaries that Joshua established for the various Israelite tribes; and the cities established for asylum and the Levitical priests.

Chapter 22 tells about a little dust-up that occurred when the eastern tribes were dismissed to return to their side of the Jordan River.

Chapter 23 contains Joshua's "farewell address" to the Israelites and his plea for them to love and remain loyal to the Lord.

Chapter 24 begins with a reminder of God's goodness and a renewal of the covenant; and then concludes with details about Joshua's death.

Joshua the Man.

Joshua the man – the son of Nun – was introduced to us in the books of Exodus, Numbers, and Deuteronomy:

- Joshua was described as Moses' "aide" (Ex 24:13), and "young assistant" (Ex 33:11); and as "a man of spirit" (Nm 27:18).

- Joshua was also a military scout (Nm 13:16) and commander. It was Joshua who mowed down Amalek and his people (Ex 17:9-13).

- Joshua was someone special to both Moses and God. Only Moses and Joshua were allowed to visit God on the mountaintop (Ex 24:13).

It appears that it was Moses who first called this son of Nun by the name of Joshua (the Hebrew pronunciation of the name "Jesus"). Both Hoshea and Joshua are variants of one original name meaning "the LORD saves."[38]

If I had to pick one verse from the Bible to describe Joshua, it wouldn't come from the books of Exodus, Numbers, Deuteronomy, or Joshua. It would be this verse from the book of Sirach:

> *Valiant leader was JOSHUA, son of Nun, assistant to Moses in the prophetic office, formed to be, as his name implies, the great savior of God's chosen ones, to punish the enemy and to win the inheritance for Israel. – Sir 46:1*

Overview of *"A Tribute to Joshua"*

One of the optional challenges at the end of my Bible study unit on Joshua (the book) was to "Present Joshua in some creative form, e.g., drawing, poem, prayer." The prayer in this chapter is the result of that challenge.

The optional challenge was somewhat vague in that it didn't distinguish between Joshua the book and Joshua the man, so I decided to limit my inspirational Scripture to the book of Joshua, while addressing Joshua the man in my prayer.

***A Tribute to Joshua* – How is it Structured?**

The book of Joshua was the source of inspiration for the prayer. None of the other verses in the Bible regarding Joshua the man were considered, including the verses previously cited from Exodus, Numbers, Deuteronomy, and Sirach.

When it was all said and done the inspirational verses came from twelve of the 24 chapters in Joshua and the prayer was divided into four sections (A-D). The focus of the prayer moved from Joshua to God as the prayer developed.

Section A provided a brief recap of Joshua's (and God's) success in conquering the "promised land."

Section B focused on Joshua's communications with the Israelites.

Section C focused on God's loyalty to Joshua.

Section D focused on God's loyalty to his people.

I have noted in the past that coming up with a name for these prayers is as difficult sometimes as writing the prayer itself. I always struggle to find that perfect name and usually fail. In this case, it wasn't quite as hard.

When my teacher returned my homework, I noted the following comment below the optional challenge: "What a marvelous tribute to Joshua!" Thus, the title for the prayer – *A Tribute to Joshua.*

So let's start out and examine *A Tribute to Joshua* – verse by verse.

Verse by Verse

A1	Lord, God, your hand is mighty.

The opening salutation notes that the Lord is mighty. The inspirational verse below connects two of God's mighty miracles – the dried-up waters in the Jordan River (Joshua) and the parting of the waters in the Red Sea (Moses).

Joshua 4:23-24 - For the LORD, your God, dried up the waters of the Jordan in front of you until you crossed over, just as the LORD, your God, had done at the Red Sea, which he dried up in front of us until we crossed over; in order that all the peoples of the earth may learn that the **hand of the LORD is mighty**, and that you may fear the LORD, your God, forever."

A2	You commanded Joshua to be firm and steadfast, to avoid the right and to avoid the left, so that he would succeed wherever he went.

In the first chapter of Joshua, God advised Joshua to "**be firm and steadfast.**"
It was an instruction to Joshua in verse 1:6.
It was identified as a primary goal ("above all") for Joshua in verse 1:7.
It was a **command** to Joshua (as prayed above) in verse 1:9.
Likewise, it is a good instruction for us as we go about our lives.

Joshua 1:7 - Above all, **be firm and steadfast**, taking care to observe the entire law which my servant Moses enjoined on you. Do not swerve from it either to the right or to the left, that you may succeed wherever you go.

A3	He acted accordingly and left nothing undone.

This verse notes that Joshua heeded the Lord's command (above) and he was successful.

Joshua 11:15 - As the LORD had commanded his servant Moses, so Moses commanded Joshua, and Joshua acted accordingly. He left nothing undone that the LORD had commanded Moses.

A4	You halted the waters of the Jordan for him;

Two miracles, as such, stood out in the book of Joshua. The verse below describes the first. The waters of the Jordan River were halted (via God's mighty hand) so that the people could cross from the eastern bank of the river to the promised land on the west bank. The Israelites were on their way. Jericho was next.

Joshua 3:15-16: No sooner had these priestly bearers of the ark waded into the waters at the edge of the Jordan, which overflows all its banks during the entire season of the harvest, than the **waters flowing from upstream halted**, backing up in a solid mass for a very great distance indeed, from Adam, a city in the direction of Zarethan; while those flowing downstream toward the Salt Sea of the Arabah disappeared entirely. Thus the people crossed over opposite Jericho.

A5	You delivered Jericho and its king to his power;
The second miracle involved the fall of Jericho. In the inspirational verse below, God informs Joshua that it is a done deal – and then provides instructions (verses 6:2-5) on the marching, blowing of horns, and shouting required to cause the city wall to collapse.	
Joshua 6:2 - And to Joshua the LORD said, "I have delivered Jericho and its king into your power.	

A6	and his fame spread throughout the land.
Joshua did as the Lord instructed. The city wall surrounding Jericho collapsed and "the people stormed the city in a frontal attack and took it" (Jos 6:20). Joshua was firm and steadfast, he acted accordingly, he succeeded, and his fame spread throughout the land. Joshua became a role model for us.	
Joshua 6:27 - Thus the LORD was with Joshua so that his fame spread throughout the land.	

B1	Joshua said to his people:
This verse sets up the bulleted verses that follow in this section. Joshua was a great communicator. Throughout the book he spoke to both his people and his enemies. Two particularly lengthy dissertations are described in chapters 23 and 24. I found the phrase "**Joshua said**" in seven of the books 24 chapters.	
Joshua 24:22 - Joshua therefore said to the people, "You are your own witnesses that you have chosen to serve the LORD." They replied, "We are, indeed!"	

B2	• Serve the Lord completely and sincerely.
Joshua was continually speaking to his people about the Lord.	
Joshua 24:14 - "Now, therefore, fear the LORD and **serve him completely and sincerely**. Cast out the gods your fathers served beyond the River and in Egypt, and serve the LORD.	

B3	• Do not be afraid or dismayed – be firm and steadfast instead.
Do you remember the phrase "be firm and steadfast" from prayer verse A2? Joshua passes on this instruction – this command – to his people.	
Joshua 10:25 - Then Joshua said to them, "**Do not be afraid or dismayed, be firm and steadfast**. This is what the LORD will do to all the enemies against whom you fight."	

B4	• **Keep the law on your lips – so that you will attain your goal.**

The inspirational verse below regarding the law was an instruction from God to Joshua. Joshua, in turn, stressed the importance of the law to his people.

Joshua 1:8 - Keep this book of the law on your lips. Recite it by day and by night, that you may observe carefully all that is written in it; then you will successfully attain your goal.

B5	• **Take great care, however, to love the Lord, your God.**

While the law was important, Joshua also instructed his people to love the Lord. In this case, the prayer verse and the inspirational verse are exactly the same.

Joshua 23:11 - Take great care, however, to love the LORD, your God.

B6	**The words of the law were read – both the blessings and the curses.**

We sometimes equate the law with the commandments (e.g., Dt 5-6). The law is also made clear via both blessings and curses.

*May you be **blessed** in the city, and **blessed** in the country!*
***Blessed** be the fruit of your womb, the produce of your soil and the offspring of your livestock, the issue of your herds and the young of your flocks! "**Blessed** be your grain bin and your kneading bowl! May you be **blessed** in your coming in, and **blessed** in your going out! – Dt 28:3-6*

***Cursed** be he who dishonors his father or his mother! …*
***Cursed** be he who misleads a blind man on his way! …*
***Cursed** be he who fails to fulfill any of the provisions of this law! … – Dt 27:16-26*

Joshua 8:34 - Then were read aloud all the words of the law, **the blessings and the curses**, exactly as written in the book of the law.

B7	**Joshua's people listened and they chose to serve you.**

This section of the prayer ends with the same inspirational verse that started it (i.e., prayer verse B1). Joshua spoke, his people listened, and they heeded his message. They chose to serve the Lord.

Joshua 24:22 - Joshua therefore said to the people, "You are your own witnesses that you have chosen to serve the LORD." They replied, "We are, indeed!"

C1	Lord, God of glory and honor:
The first line of this section on God's relationship to Joshua begins with how Joshua himself describes the God of Israel.	
Joshua 7:19 - Joshua said to Achan, "My son, give to the **LORD**, the **God of** Israel, **glory and honor** by telling me what you have done; do not hide it from me."	

C2	You did not leave or forsake Joshua.
God promised that he would not leave or forsake Joshua. "Not a single promise that the LORD made to the house of Israel was broken; every one was fulfilled" (Jos 21:45).	
Joshua 1:5 - No one can withstand you while you live. I will be with you as I was with Moses: I will not leave you nor forsake you.	

C3	Every promise you made to him was fulfilled.
As noted above.	
Joshua 23:14 - "Today, as you see, I am going the way of all men. So now acknowledge with your whole heart and soul that not one of all the promises the LORD, your God, made to you has remained unfulfilled. **Every promise has been fulfilled for you**, with not one single exception.	

C4	Joshua prayed to you and the sun stood still.
Pay attention now. This gets complicated. The main point of the inspirational passage below and the inspirational verse in C5 (Joshua 10:14), is that "**the Lord fought for Israel**."	
While Joshua and the Israelites pursued one of their enemies near Gibeon, the Lord hurled great stones from the sky [hailstones?], which killed many. At or about that time, Joshua prayed for the sun to stand still – as it had before – as recorded in the Book of Jashar. The Book of Jashar recounted **in epic style** the exploits of Israel's early heroes. In one of the epic tales in that book, the sun was halted, and the day was miraculously lengthened.	
It is probable that Joshua's prayer was likewise for an abrupt obscuration of the sun, which would impede his enemies in their flight homeward – a request that was apparently answered by the hailstorm and darkness near Gibeon.[39]	
Joshua 10:12-13: On this day, when the LORD delivered up the Amorites to the Israelites, **Joshua prayed** to the LORD, and said in the presence of Israel: Stand still, O sun, at Gibeon, O moon in the valley of Aijalon! **And the sun stood still**, and the moon stayed, while the nation took vengeance on its foes. Is this not **recorded in the Book of Jashar**? The sun halted in the middle of the sky; not for a whole day did it resume its swift course.	

C5	Never before or since was there a day like that, when the Lord obeyed the voice of a man.

The prayer verse above is very similar to the inspirational verse below. The main point for this verse and the one above is again – **the Lord fought for Israel**.

Joshua 10:14 - Never before or since was there a day like this, when the LORD obeyed the voice of a man; for **the LORD fought for Israel**.

D1	Lord, God of gods:

The God of Israel was greater than the pagan gods that their enemies worshipped in vain.

Joshua 22:22 - The **LORD, the God of gods**, knows and Israel shall know. If now we have acted out of rebellion or treachery against the LORD, our God,

D2	You gave Israel all the land that you promised. You gave them peace on every side. You brought all their enemies under their power. None of your promises were broken – everyone was fulfilled.

The prayer ends with Joshua's success. Joshua had been firm and steadfast. God's promise of land for his people was complete. The Israelites who had wandered in the desert for 40 years got the land that they were promised. This prayer was a tribute to Joshua's role in our salvation history.

We recall that Joshua is a variant of an original Hebrew name meaning "the LORD saves."

It is hard to read the prayer verse above without thinking about Israel (the country) today and the tentative peace that exists in that country and region today – thousands of years after the time of Joshua.

Joshua 21:43-45: And so the LORD gave Israel all the land he had sworn to their fathers he would give them. Once they had conquered and occupied it, the LORD gave them peace on every side, just as he had promised their fathers. Not one of their enemies could withstand them; the LORD brought all their enemies under their power. Not a single promise that the LORD made to the house of Israel was broken; every one was fulfilled.

Sacred History

Every so often, as I read the Bible, especially the Old Testament, I must remind myself (and you) that the Bible is a theological document – it tells us about God. While the Bible provides some historical facts, it is not a history book. While the Bible contains some beautiful poems, it is not a book of poetry. While the Bible even provides some cooking tips (Ex 12:8-10, Ez 4:9), it is not a cookbook.[40] The Bible is a theological document – it tells us about God.

The "Parable of the Prodigal Son" (Luke 15:11-32) tells us about God, regardless of whether the passage is a parable/story or based on historical facts. In fact, one could make the case that this parable (if that is what it is, the Bible doesn't say) tells us much more about God then many of the "historical facts" in the Bible do.

"Today historians usually recognize that there is no uninterpreted history. History is not a series of naked facts arranged in chronological order like beads on a string."[41]

When I went to high school, American history was full of uplifting stories concerning explorers like Christopher Columbus and Lewis & Clark; and our founding fathers like George Washington, Ben Franklin, and Thomas Jefferson. History then stressed facts – like the dates when documents were signed and the years that battles were fought.

Today, for whatever reason, American history is more likely to be about: Indian genocide, slavery, civil rights movements, rock and roll, Watergate, Gitmo, and gay rights. History now stresses feelings and perceived wrongs. Since dates are no longer as important, today's students struggle to arrange the chronological order of events. Most know that World War One preceded World War Two, but they will struggle to place both events on the continuum of time.

History always has and always will reflect the perspective of the person telling it, and the overall message that that historian wants to convey – the historians' bias, if you please. That bias is also evident in the historical accounts in the Old Testament. The bias of the Deuteronomic historian, whose characteristic style dominates Joshua 1-12 and the farewell address found in Joshua 23, was that the Promised Land was given to the Israelites because Yahweh, God of Israel, fought for Israel.

"For Israel, to write history was to narrate the 'mighty acts' of the Lord. … God's revelation did not come like a bolt out of the blue; it came *through* the crises and affairs of human life and *to persons* who perceived in the events a divine dimension of meaning of which the general public was unaware."[42]

Memories and Miracles

As just noted, the written history of the Israelites was their narrated memories of the mighty acts of the Lord.

If the attack on Jericho took place around 1250 BC and the Deuteronomic historian wrote his portions of Joshua around 650 BC; about 600 years transpired between the time that "the walls came tumbling down" and the recording of that event in the book of Joshua. Even if the Deuteronomic historian referenced some "crib notes" or now lost documents from that ancient era, most of what he documented were indeed memories.

"**Memory is one of man's supreme endowments.** Each of us acts today and hopes for tomorrow in the light of past experiences .... When we want to know another person, we ask him to tell us something of the story of his life, for in this way he discloses who he really is. To be a self is to have a personal history. This history is what defines one's uniqueness. In a larger sense this is true of human communities, especially those in which people are bound together primarily by shared experiences rather than natural factors like blood and soil."[43]

"The most distinctive feature of the Jewish people is their sense of history. … Indeed, if historical memory were destroyed, the Jewish community would soon dissolve. Christians, too, have this historical sense."[44]

It might help us understand the collective and historic memory of the Jewish community if we compare it to our own collective and nationalistic memories.

"In the United States, for instance, the stirring story of the Revolutionary War does not belong merely to the Thirteen Colonies or the descendents of the first colonists. Other states, joining the Union, appropriated those memories as their own. Moreover, many of us are children of immigrants who arrived on the American scene fairly late, but we too thrill to the rehearsal of the epic of early American history and affirm that this is *our* story."[45]

And in the collective and nationalistic memories of the United States you will find stories about George Washington chopping down a cherry tree and flinging a coin across the Potomac River.

Likewise, if the written history of the Israelites was their narrated memories of the mighty acts of the Lord, then they – **the Israelites – needed some mighty acts or miracles to remember**.

I don't know about you, but it is difficult for me to remember the mundane happenings of my life for a week, let alone 60 or 600 years. It is much easier for me to remember and tell others about the amazing things that happen that are exceptions to the mundane. And yes, sometimes the fish gets bigger over time.

That brings us to the miracles in the book of Joshua, like the crossing of the Jordan River and the military, albeit musical, conquest of Jericho. Incidents such as these can be viewed in several ways. They can be taken at face value as mighty deeds of the Lord done specifically to help the Israelites cross that river and conquer that city. A God who can create the universe and mankind could certainly cause these actions to occur – even if those actions conflict with our scientific conception of nature.

If we choose, we can also view these events through our understanding of nature. Some conjecture (those small notes of explanation below the biblical passages) that an earthquake caused a dam to form as the Israelites were preparing to cross the Jordan River; and/or another tremor shortly thereafter caused the weakened walls of Jericho to collapse as the Israelites were marching around the city – with or without the intervention of God.

In any case these mighty deeds or unusual happenings would be easy to remember (for six hundred years) and weave into sacred history.

It should also be noted that, "…in the Bible, miracle is something different from our conception of miracle as a disruption of natural law. As a matter of fact, the biblical writers had no conception of 'nature' as a realm for which God has ordained laws. Rather, God himself sustains his creation, and his will is expressed in natural events, whether it be the coming of the spring rains or the birth of a child. … To them an event was **wonder**-ful, or **sign**-ificant, not because it abrogated a natural law, but because it testified to God's presence and activity in their midst."[46]

Let us recap; the book of Joshua is sacred history. It contains the memories of the mighty deeds that God did for his people to help them obtain the land that he promised them. The Israelites were no longer a nomadic people wandering in the desert or looking across the Jordan into the land of the Canaanites. The Israelites were in the Promised Land. God's promise had been fulfilled.
The book of Joshua tells us about God. That is why it was written.

Warriors

"The LORD is a warrior, LORD is his name" (Ex 15:3)!

As noted above the Lord is a warrior for his people. As noted before, the Deuteronomic historians certainly believed that Yahweh, the God of Israel, fought for Israel.

The Lord is a warrior; and sometimes in salvation history he relied on other warriors to assist him. Joshua was certainly such a warrior, as documented in the book of Joshua. Throughout Old Testament times, God relied on warriors to defend his people. Some of the last recorded events in the Old Testament (as documented in 1 and 2 Maccabees) were the wars carried out by the brothers Judas, Jonathan, and Simon Maccabeus.

The need for warriors continued into Christian times. St. Paul could certainly be described as a spiritual warrior. Even some of the popes were warriors. Julius II (1503-13) has gone down in history with the title of "the warrior pope."

"[The *Book of Joshua*] is a warlike, grisly book, full of blood and violence. We tend to turn away from such a warlike book today, giving the apparently good reason that the Prince of Peace has come, and God no longer commands his people to fight bloody wars as he did then. But we are just as much at war now as then. Spiritual warfare will never end until the end; and this warfare is just as real, just as awful and as awe-full, as physical warfare. For who, after all, are more grisly: Canaanite generals or demons?"[47]

Joshua as a Type of Jesus

I introduced the concept of typology in the previous chapter and reviewed a couple of examples. In this section, I will expand my explanation of typology a bit and extend it to Joshua.

"The biblical base of typology rests on the two occurrences of the word *typos* in the Pauline writings in the sense of pattern or example. Adam is called a type of Christ (Rm 5:14); and the Israelites are called "types" for the Christian in their adventures in the desert sojourn (Ex-Num; 1 Co 10:6)."[48]

From a Bible study perspective, typological interpretations are often made to present persons, events, or institutions found in the New Testament as "types" of persons, events or institutions found in the Old Testament. These interpretations reinforce the arguments that Christ is the fulfillment of the Old Testament and that the Old Testament is part of the Christian revelation.

The resemblances between persons in the Old and New Testaments must, however, be more than merely external features in common. They must "exhibit the personal attributes of God and the nature of God's plan and will to save."[49]

"The church has traditionally interpreted Joshua as a type or symbol of Jesus for at least six reasons."[50] As you review the table below, think about how Joshua exhibits the personal attributes of Jesus, the nature of God's plan, and God's will to save his people.

Joshua	← is a type of →	Jesus
Name means "The Lord is salvation."	Name and Meaning	The Lord is our savior.
The new Moses	Relationship to Moses	The new Moses *
The conqueror of God's enemies	Role in salvation history	The ultimate conqueror of God's enemy
The one who leads his people through the waters of death (symbolized by the Jordan River).	Leadership	The one who leads his people through the waters of baptism in the New Testament (Romans 6:4).
He brings his people into the Promised Land.	Does what Moses could not do	He opens the gates of heaven for all peoples.
He divides the land for the twelve tribes.	As to "the twelve"	He expands the Church into the world via his twelve apostles.
* Moses can also be interpreted as a type of Jesus – but that is another discussion.		

Israel and Israelites

Whenever I read the Old Testament, I think of God's unique relationship with his chosen people, the people of Israel, the Israelites, and the Jews.

As noted in the *Catechism of the Catholic Church* (cf. 63, 218 and 839):
- Israel is the priestly people of God.
- God never stopped saving them.
- The gifts and the call of God are irrevocable.

"And when one considers the future, God's People of the Old Covenant and the new People of God tend towards similar goals: expectation of the coming (or the return) of the Messiah" (CCC 840).

As we ponder the above statements, we also must be cognizant of the distinctions between the people of Israel and the state of Israel. The Catholic Church, via the *Catechism* statements cited and others, notes that there is a special relationship between God and his people, and in turn between the Church and this priestly people of God.

Likewise, the United States and the country of Israel have had a long-standing and special relationship. Many fundamental and evangelical Christian denominations also have a special relationship with their Old Testament brethren and the country of Israel.

And when we consider the future, we can pray for peace in the Middle East and justice for all of God's people.

Farewell Addresses

One common element that many of the "biblical biggies" shared was their "final discourses" – their farewell addresses. In the table below, I have summarized some of these discourses, including Joshua's (as recorded in the twenty-third chapter of Joshua). These final discourses are often similar, in that they usually include some reflections on the past, foretell the future, and proclaim God's greatness.

I challenge you to read Joshua's complete discourse in the Bible.

How would your final discourse compare with Joshua's?

Would you also proclaim God's greatness – his impact on your life?

Discourse	Observation
Moses Deuteronomy 32	An instruction for all Israelites (1-3). Proclaims the greatness of God - "The Rock" (3-4). Derides the Israelites as "a perverse and crooked race" (5-6). Reflects on the good that God did for them (7-14). Foretells how Israelite sins will be punished by the pagans (15-29). Foretells how the Lord's honor will be vindicated (30-42). Moses exults and glorifies God (43).
Joshua **Joshua 23**	**An instruction for all Israel (1-2).** **Reflects on the good that God did for them (3, 9-10, 14, 15a).** **Joshua reviews what he has done to serve the Lord (4).** **Foretells what the Lord will do for them (5).** **Foretells what Israel must do, or else (6-8, 11-13, 15b, 16).**
Jacob Genesis 49	An address to his 12 sons (1-2). Proclaims the greatness of God - "the Rock of Israel" (24b-26). Foretells what is going to happen to the twelve sons (3-24a, 27).
Paul Acts 20:17-35	An address to the presbyters of the church at Ephesus (17-18). Paul reviewed how he served the Lord (18-21). Paul revealed his plan to go to Jerusalem (22). Paul foretells his future imprisonment and hardships (23-25). Paul challenges the church to be vigilant (26-31). Paul commends the Ephesians to God (32-35).
Tobit Tobit 14:3-11	An address to his son (Tobiah) and grandsons (3). Instructs them to flee because he believed God's word (4, 8). Foretells what is going to happen to Israelite kinsmen (4-8). Foretells the rebuilding of Jerusalem and temple (5). Foretells the conversion of all nations (6-7). Commands them to serve God (9). Notes benefits of almsgiving and how wickedness "kills" (10-11).

Catechism Check?

I believe that the prayer in this chapter is consistent with the *Catechism of the Catholic Church*. The preceding chapter contained additional information on typology.

We Can Pray!

We can begin our prayers by thanking God for all the people in salvation history who were, are, and will be as firm and steadfast as Joshua.

We can pray to God that we will also be firm and steadfast.

We can pray that, like Joshua, we will be God's warrior, as and when required.

We can pray that God will help us discern the spiritual battles that we need to fight – in our lives and in the culture that we live in.

We can pray to God that he helps us appreciate the Old Testament and how it is part of Christian revelation – how Jesus Christ is and was the fulfillment of the Old Testament.

We can pray for the people of Israel. We can pray for peace in the Middle East and justice for all of God's people.

At the end of my Bible study of Deuteronomy, there was an assignment to "write a final blessing which the dying Moses might have given to Joshua." Here is the blessing/prayer that I wrote at that time:

> *Lord, God, bless Joshua as he leads your people to the Promised Land.*
> *You picked Joshua to engage Amalek in battle and he mowed them down.*
> *You allowed him to climb your mountain and reside in your meeting tent.*
> *He was my aide and we trusted him.*
> *He is ready to lead your people into the Promised Land.*
> *He has said, "The Lord is with us … do not be afraid of them."*
> *Lord, God, bless Joshua as his name (Yahweh is salvation) blesses you.*

We can end our prayers by thanking God once again for Joshua and the message his name provides – "Yahweh is salvation."[51]

Chapter 5

Daniel's "Dream" Prayer

Daniel's "Dream" Prayer	Vs.	Inspiration Verse Daniel
Lord God Most High, as your angels have decreed: you rule over the kingdom of men.	A1	4:14
Lord God Most High, King of Heaven: I praise and exalt your name.	B1	4:34
As your holy sentinel showed the ancient king;	B2	4:10
it is heaven that rules over the kingdom of men.	B3	4:23
You have shown the ancient king to be shortsighted. You have shown that those who live on earth are "something," by sharing the powers of heaven through your Son with those who live and love on earth.	B4	4:32
Blessed are you Lord God Most High. Your kingdom endures through all generations.	C1	4:31
Your works are right and your ways are just.	C2	4:34

Background

This chapter is different than the rest of the chapters in this book, in that I wasn't sure that I wanted to write it. The intent of this book, via the prayers, was to write about some of the major characters in the Bible and I wasn't sure whether Daniel qualified. The prayer itself was written years ago, as part of a Bible study exercise, and it had been tucked away ever since. So I found myself with a prayer about a biblical figure named Daniel ready to go, but I wasn't sure whether Daniel met the criteria that I set for this book.

Cons:
- Daniel, in many ways is a minor biblical character – a eunuch and slave in King Nebuchadnezzar's court. He certainly wasn't Abraham, St. Paul, or Mary, the Mother of God.
- Sure he was good-looking and a vegetarian (Dn 1) but he wasn't an action hero – a warrior for God like Joshua. Daniel, for the most part, just dreamed and interpreted dreams.
- When I looked at my prayer after all the years, I noticed that only one verse was inspired by something that Daniel actually said – not much to base an entire chapter on.
- The "history" vs. "sacred history" issues were huge – the "who, what, where, why, and how" questions (e.g., was Daniel even real). Do you remember those fuzzy flowers on the cover of this book (page 6)?

Pros:
- Hey, Daniel was big enough to have a book named after him in the Bible. Not many people can say that (think Moses, King David … and you).
- My Bible study spent two weeks discussing Daniel, more time then most of the books in the Old Testament got. Someone thought Daniel was important.
- Daniel survived the lions' den once (Protestants, Dn 6) or twice (Catholics, Dn 6 and 14:31-42). God apparently thought that Daniel was important.
- I wanted to write one more chapter and **the prayer was already written**.

Taking all the above into consideration, mostly that the prayer was already written, I decided to move forward with this chapter. Daniel the man and Daniel the book will be the topic of this chapter. You can decide for yourself whether my decision was correct.

If I had to pick one verse that summarized Daniel's role in salvation history, it would be:

> *To these four young men [Daniel, Shadrach, Meshach, and Abednego]*
> *God gave knowledge and proficiency in all literature and science,*
> ***and to Daniel the understanding of all visions and dreams***. *– Dn 1:17*

Daniel the Book

Daniel is not an historical book in the sense that Joshua is. It is more of a collection of stories or, using a fancier term, "writings." The author is not identified. Most scholars seem to believe there were multiple authors.

There are basically two ways to interpret the book. Here are the choices:

> *The name "Daniel" means "God is my judge."* **He prophesied in Babylon** ... **during the Babylonian captivity [around 600 BC].** *Some of the most famous and arresting stories in the Bible are found in this book, including the three young men in Nebuchadnezzar's fiery furnace (ch. 3), the "handwriting on the wall" written by a disembodied hand, prophesying the sudden doom at King Belshazzar's feast (ch. 5), and, of course, Daniel in the lions' den (ch. 6).* **Most of the book is made up of visions of the future.**[52]

> *An examination of the material of the book ... indicates that the purpose of its composition* **[written around 165 BC]** *was to furnish consolation and encouragement for the Jews* **during the persecution of Antiochus Epiphanes.** *It is extremely probable that the author of the book did not invent the character of Daniel entirely but took a figure existing in popular tradition; and some of the book, especially the first part, may contain folklore tales of Daniel. ...* **The character of Daniel as he is presented in Dn is truly fictional.**[53]

Chapters 1-6: As noted in your first choice above, the first six chapters of Daniel are a collection of stories. Each story has a beginning, middle, and end. The stories are marvelous. They are the kinds of stories that one can easily remember, and they are great dramas.

"Purportedly telling of events that occurred in the court of Babylonia and Medo-Persia during the period of exile ... these stories are of two types: tests of loyalty (chs. 1, 3, 6) and displays of wisdom (chs. 2, 4, 5). They teach that through obedience to the law the faithful will triumph over adversity and convince foreign powers of the sovereignty of Yahweh."[54]

Chapters 7-12: The next six chapters (7-12) contain four apocalyptic visions (i.e., revelations, sometimes in the form of dreams) **of the future** – if they were written during the Babylonian exile. If they, however, were written centuries later, during the reign of Antiochus Epiphanes, they "mostly" describe **past** events.

"In this series of four visions concerning the course of world history, Daniel is not the interpreter of mysteries but rather the recipient of secret revelations."[55] In at least one case (Dn 8:27), Daniel didn't even understand his vision, in contrast to the dreams that he so easily interpreted in chapters 2 and 4.

Chapters 13-14: The last two chapters (deuterocanonical, in the Catholic Bible) contain three additional stories that involve Daniel. These stories, that stress Daniel's wisdom, are like those found in the first six chapters.

Remember once again that the Bible is not a history book. It is a theological book that tells us about God. Regardless of whether Daniel describes dreams of the future or writes of events from the past – it (the book) tells us about God.

Daniel the Man

Most of what we know about Daniel the man comes from Daniel the book. From the book of Daniel we read that:
- He was an Israelite of royal blood and of nobility (1:3).
- When he was first "placed" in the King's palace, he was young, without any defect, handsome, intelligent and wise, quick to learn and prudent in judgment (1:4).
- His "palace" name was changed to Belteshazzar (1:7).
- God gave him understanding of all visions and dreams (1:17).
- He was competent to the extent that the king made him "ruler of the whole province of Babylon" (2:48).
- He was "greatly esteemed by the people" (13:64).

Daniel is not mentioned much in the other books of the Old Testament. There is a reference to him in 1 Maccabees 2:60 – "Daniel, for his innocence, was delivered from the jaws of lions." This makes some sense since Daniel and 1 Maccabees were most likely written about the same time.

There are also some references to a "Daniel" in 1 Chronicles 3:1, Ezra 8:2, and Nehemiah 10:7 but these references provide little detail and most likely refer to others with the same name.

Likewise, there are some references to a "Daniel" in Ezekiel (14:14, 14:20 and 28:3). These verses also provide very little detail. "The Daniel named here may be the traditional just judge of the ancient past, celebrated in Canaanite literature, who is possibly reflected in Dn 13, ..."[56]

"In the late post-exilic period, when prophecy was believed to have ceased, it was common to release writings under the name of some figure of ancient Jewish tradition. In this case, the author chose the name of Daniel – a traditional, pious Israelite, according to Ezekiel ..., and a legendary hero of the Ras Shamra literature."[57]

We don't know for sure who Daniel was (e.g., palace eunuch, legendary hero, a just judge). We do know, however, that God found a role for him in salvation history.

More Background

During the fourth (and last) year of my Bible study, we spent two weeks on the book of Daniel – the first week on the "stories" found in chapters 1-6 and 13-14, the second week on the apocalyptic "visions" found in chapters 7-12.

Among the assigned exercises at the end of the first week was the following optional challenge: "Write a poem, **prayer**, or meditation based on Daniel 4." Unlike many of the other optional challenges, this one was quite specific. It focused on one chapter in Daniel – and a strange one at that.

It was strange in that it didn't involve Daniel in the lions' den, a story that one could easily meditate on. It was strange in that it didn't involve Daniel's beautiful blessing of God (2:20-23). It was strange in that it concerned a terrifying dream that King Nebuchadnezzar had. Most of the verses were the king's first-person account of that dream and subsequent events. While Daniel interpreted the dream, his involvement in the chapter was brief and limited. As such, there didn't appear to be a lot of inspirational verses to work with. This was, indeed, an optional "challenge."

Because of the nature of the challenge, I didn't have to fire up the computer search engines. All I had to do was read and reread Chapter 4, which I challenge you to do at this time. Get out that Bible and read about the "Vision of the Great Tree."

The "Vision of the Great Tree" actually starts at the end of chapter 3. The last two verses in that chapter set the stage: King Nebuchadnezzar wished all the people on Earth "abundant peace!" and then he summarized, in advance, the dream that he would go on to relate in chapter 4.

> *How great are his signs, how mighty his wonders; his kingdom is an everlasting kingdom, and his dominion endures through all generations. – Dn 3:100*

Chapter 4 is organized as follows:
- Nebuchadnezzar notes that others could not interpret his dream (1-4).
- Nebuchadnezzar graphically describes his dream for Daniel (5-15).
- Daniel interprets the dream and appeals to the king (16-24).
- Fast forward 12 months; the dream is fulfilled – and the king goes mad (25-30).
- Nebuchadnezzar's reason is restored; he praises and glorifies God, and his kingdom is restored (31-34).

The last part of chapter four became the focus of my prayer. My good news was Nebuchadnezzar's good news; as his reason was restored, as he blessed the Most High, as he prayed and glorified God.

Daniel's "Dream" Prayer - How is it Structured?

Let's take a look at this prayer. How is it structured? What are some of the key components of the prayer?

Overview

The prayer is brief, mostly because there were only thirty-four verses to work with.

The prayer is divided into three sections (A-C):

Section A is introductory in nature. Its one verse begins with a statement of adoration and ends with a brief statement of wisdom.

Section B is the heart of the prayer. It summarizes the wisdom – the reason – that King Nebuchadnezzar obtained from God.

Section C concludes the prayer. It begins with a thanksgiving blessing and ends with two statements of wisdom (from King Nebuchadnezzar).

The title of the prayer is also a little different. It connects the prayer with both Daniel the book and Daniel the man – the man who God gave "the understanding of all visions and dreams" (Dn 1:17). The prayer was inspired by both the book and the man.

So let's start out and examine *Daniel's "Dream" Prayer* - verse by verse.

Verse by Verse

A1	Lord God Most High, as your angels have decreed: you rule over the kingdom of men.

The inspirational verse below was recited by King Nebuchadnezzar as he reviewed the terrifying dream that he had.   In verse 4:10 it was noted that a holy sentinel had come down from heaven. "A holy sentinel: an angel. This term is found in the Bible only in this chapter of Daniel, but it is common in later Jewish literature."[58]
Daniel 4:14 - By decree of the sentinels is this decided, by order of the holy ones, this sentence; That all who live may know that the Most High rules over the kingdom of men: He can give it to whom he will, or set over it the lowliest of men.'

B1	Lord God Most High, King of Heaven: I praise and exalt your name.

The inspirational verse below is the last verse in Daniel 4. It concludes the "Vision of the Great Tree." It reflects the reason that was restored to King Nebuchadnezzar throughout his ordeal.

Daniel 4:34 - Therefore, I, Nebuchadnezzar, now **praise and exalt** and glorify the **King of heaven**, because all his works are right and his ways just; and those who walk in pride he is able to humble.

B2	As your holy sentinel showed the ancient king;

This prayer verse sets up the verses that follow (B3 and B4). As noted in prayer verse A1, an angel came down from heaven to show the king the truth.

Daniel 4:10 - In the vision I saw while in bed, a holy sentinel came down from heaven,

B3	it is heaven that rules over the kingdom of men.

The inspirational verse below is the only verse in this prayer that was spoken by Daniel.

Daniel 4:23 - The command that the stump and roots of the tree are to be left means that your kingdom shall be preserved for you, once you have learned **it is heaven that rules**.

B4	You have shown the ancient king to be shortsighted. You have shown that those who live on earth are "something," by sharing the powers of heaven through your Son with those who live and love on earth.

I found King Nebuchadnezzar's reasoning in the inspirational verse below to be shortsighted. The king did acknowledge the power of God. Old Testament kings could certainly understand power; but (by definition) they were not privy to the New Testament knowledge that the Church received from Jesus Christ.

Blessed with that knowledge, I radically modified the king's words to reflect the Christian message of **love** that the Church has received from "Christ the King." This knowledge became part of my prayer. Jesus assured us that we are something.

Daniel 4:32 - All who live on the earth are counted as **nothing**; he does as he pleases with the powers of heaven as well as with those **who live on the earth**. There is no one who can stay his hand or say to him, "What have you done?"

C1	**Blessed are you Lord God Most High.** **Your kingdom endures through all generations.**
	King Nebuchadnezzar's reason was restored. He acknowledges God's kingdom on Earth, a kingdom that endures through all generations, a kingdom that would endure the reign and persecution of King Antiochus Epiphanes IV, a kingdom that will endure the immorality of some of the "Obamacare" provisions.
	Daniel 4:31 - When this period was over, I, Nebuchadnezzar, raised my eyes to heaven; my reason was restored to me, and I **blessed** the **Most High**, I praised and glorified him who lives forever: His dominion is an everlasting dominion, and his **kingdom endures through all generations**.

C2	**Your works are right and your ways are just.**
	Daniel 4:34, the inspiration for prayer verse B1, also inspires the last prayer verse. It concludes the prayer as it concluded chapter 4 of Daniel and the "Vision of the Great Tree."
	Daniel 4:34 - Therefore, I, Nebuchadnezzar, now praise and exalt and glorify the King of heaven, because all his **works are right and his ways just**; and those who walk in pride he is able to humble.

Daniel's Message

The tables that follow divide Daniel (the book) into thirteen sections (usually chapters). These sections are a collection of stories and visions.

Times were tough, but God protected his people during those tough times even when they involved tyrants, fiery furnaces, and lions' dens. "The nine narratives in Daniel are tales of biblical heroes who cope successfully with difficulties, survive the terrible oppression, and in the end triumph gloriously. **In an entertaining fashion, the stories teach that good prevails over evil and that God rewards faithfulness.**"[59]

The "visions" looked back in time. "These visions have a greater historical sweep than any other in the Old Testament, and predict four great world empires: the Babylonian, the Medo-Persian, the Greek, and the Roman."[60]

Daniel the Book – Verses 1:1 - 4:34			
Passage	**Description**[61]	**Message**[62]	**Notes**
1:1-21	The Food Test	Encouraged the Jews of Maccabean times, who were forbidden by the decrees of Antiochus to observe the laws of cleanliness.	
2:1-49	The King's Dream		A
3:1-97	The Fiery Furnace	Encouraged the Jews of Maccabean times not to worship the gods of the Greeks and assures them that God will preserve them.	
3:98 – 4:34	Vision of the Great Tree	Showed that God can humble even the greatest power of the earth, which cannot recover from its fall unless it confesses.	B

Note A: Daniel 2 and Genesis 41 are very similar. The pharaoh and the king both had dreams that bothered them. Their court magicians could not interpret the dreams, but God (via Joseph and Daniel) could. The Pharaoh and the king were pleased with the interpretations and, as a result, both Joseph and Daniel were promoted to high posts in the government.

Note B: There are also some similarities between Daniel 4 and Genesis 41. In addition to those noted above in Note A (dream interpretations, promotions); both Daniel 4 (4 times) and Genesis 41 (29 times) reference the number seven (e.g., seven-year periods of time).

Daniel the Book – Verses 5:1 - 12:13			
Passage	**Description**	**Message**	**Notes**
5:1 – 6:1	The Writing on the Wall	Showed that God predicts the downfall of powers hostile to His people.	
6:2-29	In the Lions' Den	Showed that God protects His faithful in times of persecution, like those of Antiochus Epiphanes, when prayer to Yahweh was forbidden.	
7:1-28	Vision of the Four Beasts		Verse 1
8:1-27	Vision of the Ram and He-goat		Verse 2
9:1-27	Gabriel and the 70 Weeks		Verse 3
10:1 – 12:13	Vision of the Hellenistic Wars	This [10:1 – 11:45] is a prophecy *ex eventu* and is a type which appears nowhere else in the Old Testament; it is a technique of apocalyptic literature to relate contemporary events in the form of a revelation made to some hero of remote antiquity.	
		This [12:1-13] is the earliest expression of belief in the resurrection of both the righteous and the wicked.	Verse 4

Verse 1: Some view this verse as forecasting the earthly reign of Jesus Christ.

As the visions during the night continued, I [Daniel] saw one like a son of man coming, on the clouds of heaven; When he reached the Ancient One and was presented before him, he received dominion, glory, and kingship; nations and peoples of every language serve him. His dominion is an everlasting dominion that shall not be taken away, his kingship shall not be destroyed. – Dn 7:13-14

Verse 2: The little horn is Antiochus IV, and the glorious country is Palestine.[63]

Out of one of them came a little horn which kept growing toward the south, the east, and the glorious country. – Dn 8:9

Verse 3: "A threefold request (often called the Old Testament *Kyrie eleison* = 'Lord, have mercy') summarizes and concludes [Daniel's] prayer: ...."[64]

O Lord, hear! O Lord, pardon! O Lord, be attentive and act without delay, for your own sake, O my God, because this city and your people bear your name! – Dn 9:19

Verse 4: "This promise of resurrection for individual reward and punishment is nearly unparalleled in the Old Testament...."[65] "God revealed the resurrection of the dead to his people progressively. Hope in the bodily resurrection of the dead established itself as a consequence intrinsic to faith in God as creator of the whole man, soul and body" (CCC 992).

Many of those who sleep in the dust of the earth shall awake; some shall live forever, others shall be an everlasting horror and disgrace. – Dn 12:2

Daniel the Book – Verses 13:1 - 14:42			
Passage	**Description**	**Message**	**Notes**
13:1-63	*Susanna's Virtue*	An example of the wisdom of Daniel.	C
14:1-42	*Bel and the Dragon*	Daniel's escape from the lions led King Cyprus to confess that the God of Israel is the true God.	D
Italics indentify verses that are considered fully authoritative and deuterocanonical by Roman Catholics. They are not accepted as such by most, if not all, Protestant denominations.			

Note C: There are some similarities between the plight of Susanna in Daniel 13 and Joseph's temptation in Genesis 39.

Note D: Chapter 14 contains two stories. The first (1-22) concerns an idol called Bel, which Daniel destroys. The second (23-27) concerns a dragon that Daniel also destroys. Because Daniel destroyed Bel and the dragon, he was thrown into a lions' den for a second time (28-42), and for a second time he survives.

Hellenism and the Manifesto of the Hasidim (One Theory)

So how does the book of Daniel and the stories described therein equate to history generally and sacred history specifically?

Let me start to answer that question by defining a term and setting the stage by describing what was going on in the world around the time that Daniel was most likely written.

The term "**Hellenism**" is used to describe the Greek-like culture that was widespread at the time that Daniel was written. It was a culture that was bumping up against Jewish traditions. I will discuss this term in more detail later in this chapter. A Jewish sect known as the **Hasidim**, which probably evolved into the Pharisees of the New Testament, was outraged by this cultural shift and by the attempts of Antiochus Epiphanes IV to force Hellenism upon Jerusalem and Judea via his laws, edicts, and swords between 175 and 163 BC.

"Shortly after the outbreak of the Maccabean wars, an unknown writer composed the book of Daniel. Undoubtedly he was one of the Hasidim, who felt a revulsion for the ways of Hellenism and the tyranny by which it was imposed upon the Jews. His purpose was to rekindle the faith of Israel, which was in danger of being extinguished by the aggressive and severe policies of the Seleucids, and to summon the Jewish people to unyielding loyalty even in the face of prosecution. … **The book of Daniel, then, sets forth the theology of the Maccabean revolution. It has been rightly called 'the Manifesto of the Hasidim.'**"[66]

Sacred History – versus Durant's History

In the previous chapter on Joshua, I wrote about the history and "sacred history" found in the books of the Old Testament.

As noted previously, the book of Daniel contains mostly "writings" (i.e., stories, visions). But in those writings, particularly the "visions," there is both history and sacred history. In a sense, Daniel's visions supplemented the history and sacred history recorded in 1 and 2 Maccabees.

While many of the biblical authors included history in their books, so too, many historians have written about the sacred. One such historian was Will Durant, who with the help of his wife Ariel, wrote (in eleven volumes, almost 9000 pages), "The Story of Civilization." In his second volume *The Life of Greece,*[67] he wrote about Antiochus IV; Hellenism and the Jews; and the books of the Jews.

Excerpts from those writings are included in the next three sections of this chapter because they provide a wonderful background on those times. They can help you understand Daniel's visions and why the author(s) of Daniel were trying to encourage their people. Lastly, they provide an historical perspective of the Old Testament books including the book of Daniel.

As you read Durant's secular history of Antiochus IV in the next section of this chapter, compare it with the following passage from the book of Daniel, which many consider to be a description of Antiochus IV. Are the descriptions consistent? Is this sacred history indeed history?

> *… There shall arise a king, impudent and skilled in intrigue. He shall be strong and powerful, bring about fearful ruin, and succeed in his undertaking. He shall destroy powerful peoples; his cunning shall be against the holy ones, his treacherous conduct shall succeed. He shall be proud of heart and destroy many by stealth. But when he rises against the prince of princes, he shall be broken without a hand being raised. – Dn 8:23-25*

Durant's History – Antiochus IV [68]

Antiochus IV *was both the most interesting and the most erratic of his line, a rare mixture of intellect, insanity, and charm. He governed his kingdom ably despite a thousand injustices and absurdities. He allowed his delegates to abuse their power, and gave his mistress authority over three cities. He was generous and cruel without judgment, often forgiving or condemning by whim, surprising simple folk with costly gifts, and tossing money with a child's ecstasy among the crowds in the street. He loved wine, women, and art; he drank to excess, and left his royal seat, at banquets, to dance naked with the entertainers, or to carouse with wastrels; he was a Bohemian whose dream of power had come true. …*

The chief effect of his passion for things Roman was the introduction of gladiatorial games in Antioch, his capital. The people resented the brutal sport, but Antiochus won them over by lavish and spectacular displays; when they became accustomed to the butchery he considered their degeneration a personal victory. It was characteristic of him that he began as an ardent follower of the Stoics, and ended as an easy convert to the Epicureans. He enjoyed his own qualities so keenly that he labeled his coins **Antiochus Theos Epiphanes – the God Made Manifest***.*

Overreaching himself in the manner of his imaginative kind, he attempted in 169 to conquer Egypt. He was succeeding when Rome, herself a candidate for the Egyptian plum, ordered him to retire from African soil. Antiochus asked time to consider; but the Roman envoy, Popilius, drew a circle in the sand around Antiochus, and bade him decide before stepping over its line. **Antiochus yielded in fury, plundered the Temple at Jerusalem** *to restore his treasury, sought glory like his father in a campaign against the eastern tribes, and died in Persia on the way, of epilepsy, madness, or disease.*

Durant's History – Hellenism and the Jews [69]

[Note: **Chasidim** (below) is an alternative spelling of Hasidim.]

The history of Judea in the Hellenistic age turns on two conflicts: the external struggle between Seleucid Asia and Ptolemaic Egypt for Palestine, and the internal struggle between the Hellenic and Hebraic ways of life. …

Against this powerful assault upon both the intellect and the senses three forces defended the Jews:
- *the persecution under **Antiochus IV**,*
- *the protection of Rome, and*
- *the power and prestige of a Law believed to be divinely revealed. …*

*They began (about 300 B.C.) with a simple pledge to avoid wine for a given period; later, by the inevitable psychology of war, they went to the extremes of Puritanism, and frowned upon all physical pleasure as a surrender to Satan and the Greeks. The Greeks marveled at them, and classified them with the strange 'gymnosophists,' or nude ascetic philosophers, whom Alexander's army had come upon in India. Even the common Jew deprecated the severe religiosity of the **Chasidim**, and sought for some middle way. Perhaps a compromise would have been reached had it not been for the attempt of **Antiochus Epiphanes** to force Hellenism upon Judea by persuasion of the sword. …*

*… feeling their religion challenged in its very existence, the majority of the Jewish people went over to the side and view of the Chasidim. When **Antiochus IV** was expelled from Egypt by Popilius (168), the news reached Jerusalem in the form of a report that he had been killed. The rejoicing Jews deposed his appointees, massacred the leaders of the Hellenizing party, and cleansed the Temple of what they felt to be pagan abominations.*

***Antiochus**, not dead but humiliated, moneyless, and convinced that the Jews had obstructed his campaign against Egypt and were conspiring to return Judea to the Ptolemies, marched up to Jerusalem, slaughtered Jews of either sex by the thousand, desecrated and looted the Temple, appropriated for the royal coffers its golden altar, its vessels, and its treasuries, restored Menelaus to supreme power, and gave orders for the compulsory Hellenization of all Jews (167).*

You can read 1 Maccabees, in the Catholic Bible, for a continuation of this story.

Durant's History – Books of the Jews [70]

Through all the turmoil of the time the Jews maintained their traditional love of scholarship, and produced more than their share of the lasting literature of the age. To this period [322-146 BC] belong some of the finest portions of the Bible. …

By the close of the third century the scholars of the Great Assembly had completed the editing of the older literature, and had closed the canon of the Old Testament; it was their judgment that the age of the prophets was ended, and that literal inspiration had ceased. The result was that many works of this epoch, full of wisdom and beauty, lost the chance of divine collaboration, and fell into the unfortunate category of Apocrypha [or deutereocanonical, per Catholic terminology]. …

*In the **Book of Daniel** the whole terror of the age of **Antiochus IV** finds a voice. About 166, when the faithful had been persecuted to the death for their beliefs, and ever larger enemies were advancing upon the Maccabean band, one of the Chasidim, probably, undertook to rekindle the courage of the people by describing the sufferings and prophecies of Daniel in the days of Nebuchadnezzar in Babylon. Copies of the book passed secretly among the Jews; it was given out as the work of a prophet who had lived three hundred and seventy years before, had borne greater trials than any Jew under Antiochus, had emerged victorious, and had predicted a like triumph for his race. And even if the virtuous and faithful found indifferent fortune here, their reward would come at the Last Judgment, when the Lord would welcome them into a heaven of unending happiness, and plunge their persecutors into everlasting hell.*

*All in all, the extant Jewish writings of this period may be described as a mystic or imaginative literature of instruction, edification, and consolation. To the Jews of earlier ages life itself had been enough, and religion was not a flight from the world but a dramatization of morals by the poetry of faith; a powerful God, ruling and seeing all things, would reward virtue and punish vice in this existence on earth. The Captivity had shaken this belief, the restoration of the Temple had renewed it; it broke down under the bludgeoning of **Antiochus**. …*

Meanwhile Jewish contact with Persian ideas of heaven and hell, of a struggle between good and evil, and the final triumph of good, offered an escape from the philosophy of despair, and perhaps the ideas of immortality that had come down from Egypt to Alexandria, and those that had animated the mysteries of Greece, co-operated to inspire in the Jews of the Greek and Roman periods that consoling hope which bore them up through all the vicissitudes of their Temple and their state.

*From these Jews, and from the Egyptians, Persians, and Greeks, the idea of eternal reward and punishment would flow down into **a new and stronger faith**, and help it to win a disintegrating world.*

Dreams

God gave Daniel the understanding of all visions and dreams (Dn 1:17).

"Dreams are successions of images, ideas, emotions, and sensations that occur involuntarily in the mind during certain stages of sleep. The content and purpose of dreams are not definitively understood, though they have been a topic of scientific speculation, as well as a subject of philosophical and religious interest, throughout recorded history."[71]

As noted above, dreams have been of religious interest throughout recorded history. In fact the word "dream" and its derivatives (s, er, ers, ed, ing) can be found in 19 books of the Bible, mostly in the Old Testament. The most notable New Testament dreams involved Joseph, "the angel of the Lord," Mary, and baby Jesus (Mt 1-2).

The content and purpose of dreams isn't very clear – even from the Bible, as you can read in the following two beautiful passages. I took the liberty of laying out the verses in a poetic format. Try to read them accordingly.

For God does speak, *perhaps once, or even twice,* *though one perceive it not.* *In a dream, in a vision of the night,* *(when deep sleep falls upon men)* *as they slumber in their beds,* *It is then he opens the ears of men* *and as a warning to them,* *terrifies them;* *– Job 33:14-16*	*Empty and false are the hopes of the senseless,* *and fools are borne aloft by dreams.* *Like a man who catches at shadows or chases the wind,* *is the one who believes in dreams. …* *Divination, omens and dreams all are unreal;* *what you already expect, the mind depicts.* *Unless it be a vision specifically sent by the Most High,* *fix not your heart on it;* *For dreams have led many astray,* *and those who believed in them have perished.* *– Sirach 34:1-2, 5-7*

The kicker – the big question – is stated towards the end of the passage from Sirach. How do we know when a vision is specifically sent by the Most High? When is a dream from a false teacher, a false prophet, or just the result of some bad potato salad? One person who believed that he received a vision from the Most High was Joseph Faddelle.

In his book *The Price to Pay: A Muslim Risks All to Follow Christ*, Joseph Fadelle writes of the dreams that prompted him to convert to Catholicism. The book tells about how this decision resulted in imprisonment, physical attacks, and ostracism.

Joseph wrote that in May of 1987, for perhaps the first time in his life, he awoke remembering a dream. This situation – his inability to remember dreams – had concerned him to the point that he had once consulted his doctor regarding this "abnormal condition."

In his rare 1987 dream, Joseph was across a narrow stream from a beautiful man (tall, blue-gray eyes, a thin beard, medium-length hair). Joseph was impelled to jump over to the other side of the stream to meet this man but when he jumped, he found himself suspended in time for several minutes that seemed like eternity.

> *Looking at me with an infinitely kind expression, the man slowly spoke to me a single enigmatic sentence, in a reassuring and inviting tone of voice: "To cross the stream, you must eat* **the bread of life**.*"*[72]

When Joseph (a Muslim) awoke the next day, the sentence was incomprehensible but clearly engraved on his brain. Later that day, a friend – a fellow-soldier in Saddam Hussein's army, and an Iraqi Christian – gave Joseph the "Gospel" (a Bible or copy of the New Testament – the book does not say). For the first time in Joseph's life he began to read the gospels and against his friend's advice, he started with the book of John.

> *When I got to chapter 6, I stopped short, dumfounded, in the middle of a sentence. My brain was seething. For a second I thought that I was the victim of a hallucination, so I plunged again into my reading, at the precise place in the book where I had stopped. No doubt about it, I had not been mistaken. By what miracle I cannot say, but at that moment I had just read the words* **"the bread of life"**, *exactly the same words that I had heard several hours before in my dream.*[73]
>
> *... At the same moment I understood that my dream the night before had been more than a dream: there had been in it, I sensed very clearly, something like a call or a personal message that was addressed to me through those words, by whom exactly I did not know; I was incapable of saying what that man meant to me, or what the significance of all this was. All that I knew was the joy that event brought me. I was certain that from then on my life would never again be like before.*[74]

Joseph was no ordinary Muslim. He was the heir apparent to a family that traced itself back to the prophet. He struggled with his conversion experience, trying to understand what happened, trying to learn more about Christianity, trying to find a Catholic priest to help him. Because conversions to Christianity were punishable by death, help was hard to find. While he was sneaking about looking for help, his father surprised him with an arranged marriage to a Muslim women named Anwar, a woman that he didn't know. This complicated things even further.

Joseph continued to sneak about looking for help, even attending Catholic Masses from time to time. When his wife got suspicious enough to accuse him of seeing another woman, he told her the truth – and she left him, returning to her family, but not telling anyone why. Later, when Joseph had the courage to meet Anwar again, she told him the following:

> *Then I dreamed that I was in the company of several people, around* **a sort of bread***. ... There was a place for me around the table; I sat down and was about to taste the dish that they offered me, when a woman's voice interrupted me, saying, "Wash your hands before eating!" In my dream I turned around ... and I saw a very beautiful women who was carrying a jug of water. I got up then and went over to her, and she poured water for me so that I could wash my hands and face. At that moment I woke up, with my face all wet.*[75]

Joseph believed that his dream was more than a dream. In his book he never wrote that it was "a vision specifically sent by the Most High," but he acted accordingly. He acted as though God does speak, "perhaps once, or even twice" to men (and women) in their dreams. He and his wife acted accordingly.

God had opened Joseph's ears and a terrifying chapter in his life was about to begin. His book goes on to finish telling the story of his conversion, baptism, and his family's flight from Iraq. It is a terrifying story of conversion that would make a great movie. It is one of those conversion stories that can make a cradle Catholic ashamed of his lackadaisical and lukewarm faith. I encourage you to read *The Price to Pay*, for a full account of his dream and life.

Catechism Check?

I believe that the prayer in this chapter is consistent with the *Catechism of the Catholic Church*.

We Can Pray!

We can praise and exalt God's name (as in prayer verse B1).

We can thank God for Daniel – whoever and whatever he was – for what he teaches us about the kingdom of God.

We can pray that all our dreams are happy ones.

Better yet, we can pray that our dreams lead us to God.

Chapter 6

A Nativity Prayer

Prayer	Vs.	Inspiration
Almighty God, holy is your name. Your mercy is from age to age.	A1	Lk 1:49-50
I delight in the fact that nothing is impossible for you.	A2	Lk 1:37
The good news of great joy has been proclaimed for all.	A3	Lk 2:10
Blessed be you Lord. You have brought redemption to your people.	B1	Lk 1:68-70
You have given me knowledge of salvation. Because of your tender mercy, you have forgiven my sins. The daybreak from on high shines down upon me. I no longer sit in darkness and death's shadow. The daybreak guides my feet as I walk along your path.	B2	Lk 1:76-79
The virgin bore a son named Emmanuel.	C1	Mt 1:23
The shepherds glorified and praised him.	C2	Lk 2:20
The magi saw his star at its rising and came to give him homage.	C3	Mt 2:1-2
Like the heavenly multitude that suddenly appeared, I pray "Glory to God in the highest."	C4	Lk 2:13-14

Background

The second year of The Denver Catholic Biblical School Program was entitled *New Testament Foundations: Jesus and Discipleship*. After an introductory unit on how to approach the gospels, we began a four-week study of Mark's gospel.

Let me digress for a moment to discuss the three stages of gospel formation. We tend to read the gospels as if they were newspaper or magazine accounts, written at or about the time that the events took place. In actuality, biblical scholars believe that the gospel accounts were not written for many years (at least 30) after Jesus was crucified and although they are positioned first in the New Testament, some of the letters of St. Paul were most likely written before the gospels were written. So how were the gospels developed?

1. **The gospel was "lived" while Jesus was on this earth.** Others, including the apostles and disciples, saw Jesus live the "good news" of salvation.

2. **The gospel was "preached" after Jesus' resurrection.** The apostles orally described the Jesus that lived – and the Jesus that they had observed. Since the apostles were first-hand witnesses, they could describe what they saw. This very human presentation of the "gospel lived" was a great way to evangelize. Over time, others that had not witnessed Jesus' ministry first-hand also began to preach the gospel (e.g., St. Paul).

3. **The gospel was "written" after it became very apparent that Jesus was not coming "soon."** The gospels of Matthew, Mark, Luke, and John were written to remember the past, to develop and clarify doctrine, and to communicate with an increasingly geographically dispersed church.

So how did I feel after studying Mark's gospel for four weeks?

To be honest, Mark's gospel didn't give me a bunch of warm and fuzzy feelings. I enjoyed the parables, as I liked that literary style and teaching technique. Mark crammed a lot of action into his relatively brief gospel, but he didn't develop his "characters" very well. Above all, I was disappointed in the way Jesus treated his disciples and his family. If twelve-plus men who followed Jesus for months couldn't get it, what hope was there for me? Was I just another "insider" on the outside? Was I just one more to be added to the list of the Godforsaken?

But we should not forget what Mark knew (because he wrote it down) that he was just writing "the beginning of the gospel of Jesus Christ" (Mk 1:1).

More Background

Anyway, after four weeks of Mark we were set to move on – but to move on to what? It turned out that the gospel of Luke was scheduled to be the next major topic. Three weeks (units 7-9) would be devoted to Luke but something special was scheduled for the week (unit 6) between Mark and Luke. That "something special" was the **infancy narratives** (found in the first two chapters of both Matthew and Luke).

The first gospel written had skipped Jesus' birth. Mark had started out with the preaching of John the Baptist. A mature Jesus happened along soon after and was baptized by John the Baptist (Mk 1:9). There was no infancy narrative in Mark.

Likewise, the gospel of John, with its high Christology, had no infancy narrative. In John, "the Word became flesh" (John 1:14) but not with a lot of detail (no magi, no star, no shepherds).

Only Matthew and Luke bothered to tell us about Jesus' birth and their stories emphasized different aspects of his birth.

So anyway, the two optional challenges listed in the workbook for Unit 6 were:[76]

1. Express the "atmosphere" created by **each infancy narrative** in some prayer or art form (i.e., express the overall "feeling" and "attitude" as you perceive it in each version).

2. Depict **each "Christmas" story** in an art or prayer form.

As I have noted before, "art" and "art forms" are not my thing, so I chose to write a prayer regarding the infancy narratives – regarding the Christmas stories. I deviated from the challenge to the extent that I did not write about "each" of the narratives – about "each" of the stories. I took them both on at the same time and ended up with one prayer – *A Nativity Prayer*.

More on the "Synoptic" Gospels

Before I take on *A Nativity Prayer*, I would like to spend a little more time on the synoptic – the similar – gospels. I think that this time will help us understand the Christmas stories better. The table below provides some information on the gospels of Mark, Luke, and Matthew.[77] Almost all the entries are "best guesses" or opinions. They may or may not be accurate.

Gospel →	Mark	Luke	Matthew
Author	John Mark? assistant to Paul, Barnabas, and perhaps Peter	Luke - an "artist in words"	Matthew Levi - a tax collector - one of the 12 disciples
Author's background	Jew Pro Peter? Anti Paul?	Antiochian Gentile Friend of Paul Physician?	Jew
Language	Greek with Latinisms	Excellent Greek	Greek
Written at	Rome?	Not from Palestine Member of Antioch church?	Antioch?
Audience	The terse, clear, pointed style would appeal to unevangelized Romans.	The larger Graeco-Roman world	Matthean church in Syria Christians of Jewish background
Emphasis	The human side and work of Jesus. Expect suffering! Mark is a gospel of action and miracles.	Salvation Doctrine Holy Spirit Women / children	The Kingdom of Heaven
Special Features	The Son of God is also the servant of God.	The Magnificat The Benedictus Gloria in Excelsis Nunc Dimittis	Matthew is the Gospel of: - discourse - the Church - the King

The synoptic gospels were written many years after Christ was crucified and they were written by men of different backgrounds to different audiences – so that all would know the truth concerning the matters which they had been or would be instructed. God's "truth" was the same, but the emphasis was different.

The Homogenized Nativity Story

As noted previously the gospels of Mark and John did not have nativity stories. That leaves Matthew (written by a Jew to Christians with Jewish backgrounds) and Luke (written by a Gentile to the larger Graeco-Roman world) as the only gospels with nativity stories.

As you proceed with this chapter and/or read the nativity accounts in Matthew and Luke, you may wish to get out your nativity set. Get out the manger, the sheep, the shepherds, and the magi. Get out Joseph, Mary, the baby Jesus. If your nativity set came with a star, bring it out.

As we proceed, you will note that you do not need all the pieces as you read Matthew. Likewise, you will not need all the figurines as you read Luke. Only when you homogenize the two accounts (as we have in our minds since we were kids) do you need all the pieces. We will discuss these differences as we proceed. The tables on the following pages will hopefully help you understand these differences. The tables provide summaries of what both Luke and Matthew were trying to emphasize in their narratives – to their audiences.

Both writers were acknowledging what we sometimes forget – that Jesus was a Jew. Note how both writers positively stress Jesus' Jewish roots as they expand Jesus' reach to the Gentiles – via the gifts of the magi in Matthew – and the gratitude suggested in Luke.

Before proceeding on to the prayer and its verses, I would recommend that you get out your Bible (and nativity set) and read the first two chapters of Matthew and the first two chapters of Luke. Try to keep the two accounts separate for now. Try to read the accounts from the perspective of the authors and their first century audiences.

Emphasis of Matthew's Infancy Narrative: [78]	
Matthew emphasizes continuity with the Old Testament, which was very sacred to the Jews. • modeled on baby Mose's story • Jesus is the new Moses	Matthew is writing primarily to Jewish Christians who were experiencing a terrible religious crisis (i.e., they were excommunicated Jews). Their whole world was turned topsy-turvy.
	Matthew's secondary audience was the recent Gentile converts in the Jewish-Christian community.
Thus: Matthew's goal was to reassure his readers that they had not lost their heritage as Jews.	**Examples:** • Jesus' Jewish ancestry, with references to the strange and unexpected maternal connections, is reported. • The infancy narrative begins with Joseph, a respectable Jew, who willingly accepts Mary as his wife AFTER an angel assures him. • Jesus was born in the Jewish town of Bethlehem. • There is a quote from the OT.
	• Only the Gentile Magi, guided by their star, welcomed Jesus. • Jesus fled to safety in Gentile Egypt.
But: The mood of Matthew reflected the mood of the early Jewish Christians that all Jews had gathered forces against them.	**Examples:** • Even Joseph didn't initially welcome the news that Jesus would be born. • No Jews welcomed Jesus when he was born (i.e., Jesus seems to have been excommunicated also). • The OT quote from Jeremiah noted the topsy-turvy world of Rachel and her lamentation. • The Jewish king and the Sanhedrin try to kill Jesus and the "innocents."

Emphasis of Luke's Infancy Narrative:	
Luke emphasizes the wonderful news of salvation, that the Gentiles were now part of, because: • Jesus was a Jew. • Jews, including many women, had raised and supported Jesus during his ministry. • Jewish missionaries had converted the Gentiles.	Luke is a Gentile, writing for mainly Gentile readers, who are hardly aware of the identify crisis that the Jewish Christians were experiencing.
Thus: Luke wants to teach his readers to look back with reverent **gratitude** to the Jewish people, including the women who were instrumental in Jesus' ministry.	**Examples:** • Angels told Zechariah and Mary of the coming of Jesus (just as the Jewish missionaries had told the Gentiles about Jesus). • All the Jews in Luke's infancy narrative (e.g., Elizabeth, the shepherds, Simeon, Anna) are beautiful, Spirit-filled people, eagerly expecting the Messiah and welcoming him with love and joy. • Luke notes the Jewish temple and purification rites and connects Jesus' birth with Jewish scripture. • From Luke, we learn that Mary's greatness comes from her spiritual greatness. • Luke stresses prayer (**gratitude**). • Luke stresses the poverty to which the Gentile Christians are called. Only the poor shepherds come to honor baby Jesus.

A Nativity Prayer - How is it Structured?

Let's take a look at *A Nativity Prayer*. How is it structured? What are some of the key components of the prayer?

Overview

The prayer is relatively short. All the inspirational verses were selected from the nativity stories in Luke 1-2 and Matthew 1-2. As it turned out, only two of the prayer verses were inspired by Matthew. The remainder of the prayer came from the more lyrical nativity account found in Luke.

The prayer was arranged into three sections as noted below:

Section A consists primarily of adoration and praise. It associates an almighty God with mercy. This is the good news of great joy proclaimed.

Sections B thanks God for the redemption that he brought to us via Jesus.

Sections C starts out with three statements of wisdom regarding Jesus' birth and then concludes with a final adoration.

A Nativity Prayer is one of the few prayers that I have written that contains no petitions, no lamentations, and no requests for intercession. When I started to write the prayer, I had no such goal. The prayer just developed in that direction. This emphasis on adoration, praise, and thanksgiving should probably not have surprised me though – after all the nativity stories in Luke and Matthew involved the birth of a baby.

What do you do when you "visit" a hospital maternity unit? I suspect that you are there to praise and adore. And even though the baby Jesus was God (and the shepherds and Magi knew it), it did not seem appropriate to petition a baby. It was a time to be thankful – a time to adore and praise.

Verse by Verse

A1	Almighty God, holy is your name. Your mercy is from age to age.
"Faithful to the witness of Scripture, the Church often addresses its prayer to the **'almighty** and eternal God' … believing firmly that **'nothing will be impossible with God'"** (CCC 276).	
Luke 1:49-50: The Mighty One has done great things for me, and holy is his name. His mercy is from age to age to those who fear him.	

A2	I delight in the fact that nothing is impossible for you.
The *Catechism* notes that the Holy Scriptures repeatedly remind us of the universal power of God. It should not surprise us that God is **almighty** in heaven and on earth since God created heaven and earth and **nothing is impossible with God**, who disposes his works according to his will (cf. CCC 269).	
Luke 1:37 - for nothing will be impossible for God."	

A3	The good news of great joy has been proclaimed for all.
"In the faith of his humble handmaid, the Gift of God found the acceptance he had awaited from the beginning of time. She whom the **Almighty** made 'full of grace' responds by offering her whole being: 'Behold I am the handmaid of the Lord; let it be (done) to me according to your word'" (CCC 2617). Don't miss the connections in this section of the prayer: • The good news of great joy was proclaimed because Mary accepted. • The almighty God made Mary "full of grace." • The good news was proclaimed for all. Would you have expected less from an almighty God? The Catholic Church holds Mary in high esteem – primarily because of the verses recorded in the nativity accounts. Later in this chapter, I will address in more detail what we learn about Mary in these four chapters from Matthew and Luke.	
Luke 2:10 - The angel said to them, "Do not be afraid; for behold, I proclaim to you good news of great joy that will be for all the people.	

B1	**Blessed be you Lord.** **You have brought redemption to your people.**
From the perspective of all mankind, this is the good news. God, as promised by the prophets, has brought redemption to his people – and all God's people (should) say, Amen!	
Luke 1:68-70: "Blessed be the Lord, the God of Israel, for he has visited and brought redemption to his people. He has raised up a horn for our salvation within the house of David his servant, even as he promised through the mouth of his holy prophets from of old:	

B2	**You have given me knowledge of salvation.** **Because of your tender mercy, you have forgiven my sins.** **The daybreak from on high shines down upon me.** **I no longer sit in darkness and death's shadow.** **The daybreak guides my feet as I walk along your path.**
The inspirational verse from Luke has such beautiful imagery. How could one not incorporate this verse into a prayer? It speaks of salvation. It speaks of God's mercy. The references to daybreak and the guiding hand along the path are beautiful. The reference to "death's shadow" jumps out from the page. It becomes the New Testament equivalent to Psalm 23. The light of the daybreak penetrates the dark valley – Jesus is the light that penetrates the valley of the shadow of death.	
Luke 1:76-79: And you, child, will be called prophet of the Most High, for you will go before the Lord to prepare his ways, to give his people knowledge of salvation through the forgiveness of their sins, because of the tender mercy of our God by which the daybreak from on high will visit us to shine on those who sit in darkness and death's shadow, to guide our feet into the path of peace."	

C1	**The virgin bore a son named Emmanuel.**
Emmanuel, meaning "God is with us" or "may God be with us," was the name given by Isaiah to the infant whose birth was announced in Is 7:10-17. In the verse below, Matthew may be using the word in much the same sense that Isaiah was using it – as a prediction of the birth of an heir to the Davidic dynasty and the salvation that would be attained by David's heir – by Jesus.[79]	
Matthew 1:23 - "Behold, the virgin shall be with child and bear a son, and they shall name him Emmanuel," which means "God is with us."	

C2	The shepherds glorified and praised him.

If you reread the nativity accounts in Matthew and Luke, you may have noted that the visit of the shepherds is noted only in Luke. Like this prayer, the shepherds glorified and praised baby Jesus.

Luke 2:20 - Then the shepherds returned, glorifying and praising God for all they had heard and seen, just as it had been told to them.

C3	The magi saw his star at its rising and came to give him homage.

The visit of the magi is noted only in Matthew. Like this prayer, the magi paid homage to the baby Jesus.

As used in Matthew, the term "magi" refers to "possessors of occult knowledge" or by implication (the star) to "astrologers." The story of the magi is primarily theological in interest and purpose. Jesus, the King-Messiah, is recognized by the Gentiles but not by his own people.[80]

Through Mary, the Holy Spirit begins to bring men, the objects of God's merciful love, *into communion* with Christ. Note further how the humble are always the first to accept him: starting with the shepherds and the magi; Simeon and Anna; the bride and groom at Cana; and the first disciples (cf. CCC 725).

Matthew 2:1-2: When Jesus was born in Bethlehem of Judea, in the days of King Herod, behold, magi from the east arrived in Jerusalem, saying, "Where is the newborn king of the Jews? We saw his star at its rising and have come to do him homage."

C4	Like the heavenly multitude that suddenly appeared, I pray "Glory to God in the highest."

The prayer ends with angelic words of adoration.

"From the Incarnation to the Ascension, the life of the Word incarnate is surrounded by the adoration and service of angels. ... Their song of praise at the birth of Christ has not ceased resounding in the Church's praise: 'Glory to God in the highest!'" (CCC 333).

Luke 2:13-14: And suddenly there was a multitude of the heavenly host with the angel, praising God and saying: "Glory to God in the highest and on earth peace to those on whom his favor rests."

More Differences

The table below highlights more of the differences between the nativity accounts in Matthew and Luke. It should be stressed that the two accounts do not necessarily conflict. Matthew and Luke, for whatever reasons, may have just decided to concentrate on different parts of the same story.

Questions	Luke	Matthew
To whom did God send a message about the birth of a child?	Zechariah: - Elizabeth's husband, - John the Baptist's father Mary	Joseph
Who comes to honor the newborn child?	Shepherds	Magi from the east
What events occur in the temple?	Purification Testimonies from Simeon and Anna	*Assembling all the chief priests and the scribes of the people [**in the temple?**], he [Herod] inquired of them where the Messiah was to be born. – Mt 2:4*
What women play a part in the story?	Elizabeth, **Mary** Anna	Tamar Rahab Ruth Bathsheba **Mary** Rachel

Do you find these familiar Christmas images in these chapters?		
• the star	**No**	**Yes**
• the angels singing "Glory to God in the highest"	**Yes**	**No**
• the manger	**Yes**	**No** (on entering the house)
• the wise men's camels	**No**	**No**
• the ox and the ass	**No**	**No**
• the "three kings"	**No**	**No** - Matthew's magi were astrologers.
• the flight into Egypt	**No**	**Yes**
• the slaughter of children by Herod	**No**	**Yes**

So where did the camels, oxen, and kings that are part of our homogenized nativity account come from? Well, the animals are logical extensions of the stories. You would expect to find animals around a manger. Likewise, one might expect magi to travel on camels. The camels and the kings may have also come from the Old Testament nativity verses that have been homogenized into the New Testament nativity scenes. I will write more of this later in this chapter.

Even after reading the two nativity accounts it can be difficult to separate them from the homogenized account in our minds – from the nativity set picture that we have developed over the years.

After I read Matthew's account for the third or fourth time it finally donned on me how little Matthew had to say about the day that Christ was born. The only reference to that day comes in the last verse in chapter 1: "[Joseph] had no relations with her *until she bore a son*, and he named him Jesus." That's it! There is no manger, no baby wrapped in swaddling clothes.

In chapter 2, Matthew moves right on to the visit of the magi. It is probably because of this quick movement – from birth to magi – and because of those nativity sets (shepherds and magi huddled around the manger) that I have always thought that the magi were in Bethlehem the day that Jesus was born.

If you read Matthew's account closely, however, you will note that a lot of time transpires (i.e., a lot of things happened, a lot of travel took place) between Jesus' birth and the appearance of the magi. Would you believe that as much as **two years** transpired? In Mt 2:16, we read how Herod "ordered the massacre of all the boys in Bethlehem and its vicinity **two years** old and under, in accordance with the time he had ascertained from the magi."

It would be easy to get hung up on all the differences between the two accounts. I only bring them up to get you to try to un-homogenize (as if that were possible) the two nativity accounts so that you can develop an appreciation of the theology that each writer was trying to convey to his readers. What was each writer trying to tell you about God – about Jesus Christ?

Luke writes in imitation of Old Testament birth stories, combining historical and legendary details, literary ornamentation, and interpretation of scripture, to tell us about Jesus Christ. Luke announces many of the themes that will become prominent in the rest of his gospel:
- the centrality of Jerusalem and the temple,
- the journey motif,
- the universality of salvation,
- joy and peace,
- concern for the lowly,
- the importance of women,
- the presentation of Jesus as savior,
- Spirit-guided revelation and prophecy, and
- the fulfillment of Old Testament promises.[81]

Matthew presents the coming of Jesus as the climax of Israel's history and the fulfillment of Old Testament prophecy. Matthew portrays Jesus:

- reliving the Exodus experience of Israel,
- reliving the persecutions of Moses,
- being rejected by his own people ("all Jerusalem"),
- being accepted by the Gentiles (the "magi"),
- as the savior of his people, and
- as Emmanuel ("God is with us").[82]

The Old Testament Nativity Accounts

As noted, both Matthew and Luke connect their nativity accounts to the Old Testament. Note in the following table how Matthew uses a genealogy; past sayings by the prophets; the life of Moses; and references to stars, gold, and frankincense to connect the birth of Jesus to the Old Testament. If you examine Luke closely, you will note more connections. Although their reasons were different, both Matthew and Luke wanted to demonstrate Jesus' Jewish roots.

Connections Between Matthews Nativity Account		and the Old Testament
Mt 1:1-17	The genealogy of Jesus, per Matthew, connects Jesus to the generations from Abraham to "the Messiah."	**Note** the unusual maternal references to Tamar, Rahab, Ruth, and "the wife of Uriah" (Bathsheba).
Mt 1:23	*Behold, the virgin shall be with child and bear a son, and they shall name him Emmanuel, …*	All this took place to fulfill what the Lord had said through the **prophet** (in Isaiah 7:14).
Mt 2:2	*… Where is the newborn king of the Jews? We saw his **star** at its rising and have come to do him homage.*	*… A **star** shall advance from Jacob, and a staff shall rise from Israel, … – Nm 24:17*
Mt 2:6	*And you, Bethlehem, land of Judah, are by no means least among the rulers of Judah; since from you shall come a ruler, who is to shepherd my people Israel.*	As has been written through the **prophet** (in Micah 5:1).
Mt 2:11	*… [The magi] prostrated themselves and did him homage. Then they opened their treasures and offered him gifts of **gold, frankincense**, and myrrh.*	*Caravans of **camels** shall fill you, … All from Sheba shall come bearing **gold** and **frankincense**, and proclaiming the praises of the LORD. – Isaiah 60:6*

Connections Between Matthews Nativity Account		and the Old Testament (cont.)
Mt 2:14	*Joseph rose and took the child and his mother by night and departed for Egypt.*	He stayed there until the death of Herod, that what the Lord had said through the **prophet** Hosea (Hos 11:1) might be fulfilled: *"Out of Egypt I called my son."*
Mt 2:18	*A voice was heard in Ramah, sobbing and loud lamentation; Rachel weeping for her children, and she would not be consoled, since they were no more.*	As was said through the **prophet** Jeremiah (in Jeremiah 31:15).
Mt 2:19-20	*When Herod had died, behold, the angel of the Lord appeared in a dream to Joseph in Egypt and said, "Rise, take the child and his mother and go to the land of Israel, for those who sought the child's life are dead."*	**Note** the similarity to Ex 4:19: *In Midian the LORD said to Moses, "Go back to Egypt, for all the men who sought your life are dead."*
Mt 2:23	*[After leaving Egypt, Joseph and his family] went and dwelt in a town called Nazareth,* →	← *so that what had been spoken through the **prophets** might be fulfilled, "He shall be called a Nazorean."*

The town of Nazareth is not mentioned in the Old Testament, and no such prophecy can be found there. The vague expression "through the prophets" may be due to Matthew's seeing a connection between Nazareth and certain texts in which there are words with a remote similarity to the name of that town (e.g.,

- In Isaiah 11:1 where the Davidic king of the future is called "a bud" (**neser**) that shall blossom from the roots of Jesse,

- In Judges 13:5-7 where Samson, the future deliverer of Israel from the Philistines, is called one who shall be consecrated (a **nazir**) to God.[83]

Hail Mary - Just His Mother?

It would be easy to get hung up on the differences in the two nativity accounts and the connections between them and the promises of the Old Testament. We should probably focus instead on what each writer is trying to tell us about God – about Jesus Christ – and, may I suggest, about Jesus' mother.

What were the writers trying to tell us about Mary?

The first two chapters of Matthew and especially the first two chapters of Luke tell us a great deal about Mary. Well, to be more accurate, these four chapters tell us a great deal more about Mary than the rest of the Bible does. Matthew, via its placement in the New Testament, provides us with our first information on Mary (as noted in the table below).

What Matthew tells us about Mary	
1:16	*Jacob the father of Joseph, the husband of **Mary**.* *Of **her** was born Jesus who is called the Messiah.*
1:18	*Now this is how the birth of Jesus Christ came about.* *When his mother **Mary** was betrothed to Joseph, but before they lived together, **she** was found with child through the holy Spirit.*
1:19	*Joseph her husband, since he was a righteous man,* *yet unwilling to expose **her** to shame, decided to divorce **her** quietly.*
1:20	*Such was his intention when, behold, the angel of the Lord appeared to him in a dream and said, "Joseph, son of David, do not be afraid to take **Mary your wife** into your home. For it is through the holy Spirit that this child has been conceived in **her**.*
1:21	***She** will bear a son and you are to name him Jesus,* *because he will save his people from their sins."*
1:22-23	*All this took place to fulfill what the Lord had said through the prophet:* *"Behold, **the virgin** shall be with child and bear a son, and they shall name him Emmanuel," which means "God is with us."*
1:24	*When Joseph awoke, he did as the angel of the Lord had commanded him and took his **wife** into his home.*
1:25	*He had no relations with **her** until **she** bore a son, and he named him Jesus.*
2:11	*and on entering the house [the magi] saw the child with **Mary his mother**. They prostrated themselves and did him homage. Then they opened their treasures and offered him gifts of gold, frankincense, and myrrh.*

What Matthew tells us about Mary (continued)	
2:13	*When [the magi] had departed, behold, the angel of the Lord appeared to Joseph in a dream and said, "Rise, take the child and **his mother**, flee to Egypt, and stay there until I tell you. Herod is going to search for the child to destroy him."*
2:14	*Joseph rose and took the child and **his mother** by night and departed for Egypt.*
2:19-20	*When Herod had died, behold, the angel of the Lord appeared in a dream to Joseph in Egypt and said, "Rise, take the child and **his mother** and go to the land of Israel, for those who sought the child's life are dead."*
2:21	*He rose, took the child and **his mother**, and went to the land of Israel.*

That's it! We get a little "Maryology" in chapter 1 but not much "Maryology" (except "his mother") in chapter 2. While it is apparent that Joseph is the star of Matthew's gospel; we do find out about the role of the holy Spirit in the birth of Jesus (1:18 and 1:20) and about Mary's status as a virgin (1:22-23). We also learn from verse 1:25 and numerous verses in chapter 2, that Mary was indeed the mother of Jesus – and thus the mother of God.

Matthew's gospel has a strange start – a strange and unorthodox genealogy. The first seventeen verses in chapter 1 describe the 42 ("14" times 3) generations from Abraham to the Messiah. If you examine the genealogy closely you will note several odd things (e.g., the numbers don't add up, some Jewish kings are missing, and at least one name appears to be incorrect).

What is stranger however is the reference to "women" in the genealogy, and some unique women at that. Most biblical genealogies are very much male oriented. And check out the women listed:

- **Tamar** (Genesis 38),
- **Rahab** (Joshua 2:1-21, Joshua 6:17-25),
- **Ruth** (Ruth 1 - 4), and
- **Bathsheba** – the wife of Uriah (2 Samuel 11 - 12, 1 Kings 1 - 2).

All four women "bore their sons through unions that were in varying degrees strange and unexpected. These 'irregularities' culminate in the supreme 'irregularity' of the Messiah's birth of a virgin mother; **the age of fulfillment is inaugurated by a creative act of God.**"[84]

Hail Mary - Full of Grace

So, as we just read, Matthew set the tone. Matthew tells us that something supreme, something irregular, and something creative happened. Matthew adds a few more introductory details and then Luke takes over, in recording for us the inspired word of God.

One of the first things that stands out when one reads Luke is that the "Hail Mary" – that beloved Catholic prayer – is embedded in Luke 1-2. In these verses Luke tells us Catholics that Mary is blessed.

	Luke's "Hail Mary"	
Lk 1:26-28	*In the sixth month, the angel Gabriel was sent from God to a town of Galilee called Nazareth, to a virgin betrothed to a man named Joseph, of the house of David, and the virgin's name was **Mary**. And coming to her, he said, "**Hail, favored one! The Lord is with you.**"*	**Hail Mary, full of Grace, the Lord is with you.**
Lk 1:41-42	*When Elizabeth heard Mary's greeting, the infant leaped in her womb, and Elizabeth, filled with the holy Spirit, cried out in a loud voice and said, "Most **blessed are you among women, and blessed is the fruit of your womb**.*	**Blessed art thou among women and blessed is the fruit of thy womb,**
Lk 2:21	*When eight days were completed for his circumcision, he was named **Jesus**, the name given him by the angel before he was conceived in the womb.*	**Jesus**
Lk 2:6-7	*While they were there, the time came for her to have her child, and **she gave birth to her firstborn son**. She wrapped him in swaddling clothes and laid him in a manger, because there was no room for them in the inn.*	**Holy Mary, mother of God,**
The prayer ends with our prayer for Mary's intercession.		**pray for us sinners, now and at the hour of our death.** **Amen**

"In the faith of his humble handmaid, the Gift of God found the acceptance he had awaited from the beginning of time" (CCC 2617).

More Mary Scripture

Luke adds substantially to the basic information supplied by Matthew. I will not attempt to cite every time Mary is mentioned in Luke – as I did a few pages back with Matthew. I will, however, cite a few verses, from Luke and others, which support the Marian doctrines of the Church.

Lk 1:46-50	*And Mary said: "My soul proclaims the greatness of the Lord; my spirit rejoices in God my savior.* *For he has looked upon his handmaid's lowliness; behold, from now on will all ages call me blessed.* ***The Mighty One has done great things for me****, and holy is his name. His mercy is from age to age to those who fear him."*	**The "Magnificat"**
John 2:3-5	*When the wine ran short, the mother of Jesus said to him, "They have no wine." (And) Jesus said to her, "Woman, how does your concern affect me? My hour has not yet come." His mother said to the servers, "Do whatever he tells you."*	**Mary intercedes** at the wedding at Cana.
John 19: 26-27	*When Jesus saw his mother and the disciple there whom he loved, he said to his mother, "Woman, behold, your son."* *Then he said to the disciple, "Behold, your mother." And from that hour the disciple took her into his home.*	Before he dies, Jesus tells his beloved disciple **(and us?)** to "Behold, your mother."
Rv 11:19 - Rv 12:2	*Then God's temple in heaven was opened, and **the ark of his covenant could be seen** in the temple. There were flashes of lightning, rumblings, and peals of thunder, an earthquake, and a violent hailstorm.* ***A great sign appeared in the sky, a woman*** *clothed with the sun, with the moon under her feet, and on her head a crown of twelve stars. She was with child and wailed aloud in pain as she labored to give birth.*	The ark of his covenant … **[See page 59.]** a woman clothed with the sun … could be seen.
Mt 16: 17-19	Jesus said to him in reply, "Blessed are you, Simon son of Jonah. For flesh and blood has not revealed this to you, but my heavenly Father. And so I say to you, you are Peter, and upon this rock I will build my church, and the gates of the netherworld shall not prevail against it. I will give you the **keys** to the kingdom of heaven." …	Jesus' gives Peter the keys to the kingdom of heaven. This is the **key** to all Church Marian doctrines.

Marian Doctrines

Before getting too far into this section, let us review what the Church's Marian doctrines are. The table below provides a summary of them, with some corresponding references to the articles of the *Catechism* that are associated with the doctrines.

Doctrine	Statement of Doctrine	CCC
The Immaculate Conception	"… Mary, 'in the first instant of **her** conception was, by a singular grace and privilege of Almighty God in view of the merits of Jesus Christ, the savior of the human race, preserved exempt from all stain of original sin.'"[85]	**491** 508
The Assumption	"… Mary, 'after the completion of her earthly life' – note the silence regarding her death – '**was assumed** body and soul into the glory of Heaven.'"[86]	**966**
The Mother of God	Mary was the Theotokos (God-bearer). Mary was the "Mother of God" (not just the "Mother of Christ").	**466** 495 509
Mary as Mediatrix	By her constant intercession, Mary continues to bring us the gifts of eternal salvation. By her maternal charity, she cares for the brethren of her Son. Note: This neither takes away from nor adds anything to the dignity and efficaciousness of Christ the one Mediator.[87]	**969**
Mary's Perpetual Virginity	Mary "remained a virgin in conceiving her Son, a virgin in giving birth to him, a virgin in carrying him, a virgin in nursing him at her breast, always a virgin."[88]	**499** 510

Marian Doctrine - An Apologetic Perspective

I am not going to attempt to fully explain or rigorously defend the Marian doctrines. There are many other resources available, in addition to the *Catechism* that can do that better than I can, and it is beyond the scope of this book. From an apologetic perspective, I found Karl Keating's "Marian Beliefs" chapter in *Catholicism and Fundamentalism* to be most helpful. In 22 pages, Keating clearly explains the Marian doctrines and the "veneration" that Catholics show Mary.[89]

Apologetics is the branch of theology that attempts to explain and defend the doctrines of one's faith. The apostles were some of the first apologists. Acts 17:22-34 gives us a good example of apologetics in practice as St. Paul explains and defends the faith at the Areopagus in Athens.

Marian doctrines are not as easy to explain and defend as many other Church doctrines are. The doctrines are steeped in centuries of emotion and, relatively speaking, there are not a lot of clear scriptural passages on the topic. This latter situation is a major impediment when addressing those Christians that rely strictly on Scripture (versus Scripture and Tradition).

The Catholic Church has experienced 2000 plus years of tradition – some occurring before the Bible canon was formalized. We have the writings of the early Church fathers and the decisions of numerous councils, synods, and popes that were promulgated over the centuries to help us understand what God has revealed to us.

From an apologetic perspective, it is helpful – indeed almost mandatory – to address the development of Scripture and the structure of the Church before addressing the Marian doctrines. The remainder of this chapter will make more sense if you appreciate how the Bible canon was established and the structure (e.g., hierarchy, Magisterium) of the Church. As such, I suggest that you read or reread Chapter 3 (... Scripture ...) in the first volume of this series.

In any case, since this book is about prayer and Scripture, I feel the need to briefly discuss the Marian doctrines – as they relate to the genealogy of Jesus recorded in Matthew (1:1-17) and the other verses that I cited earlier:

- Matthew told us that something special was going to happen (Mt 1:1-17).
- Luke provided the details of the Annunciation.
- John shed light on Mary's 1.) intercessory role, 2.) in the Church.
- Revelation shed more light on the "Ark of the Covenant."
- Matthew told us about Peter's special role (to bind) in the Church.

Let me add some meat to the bones – let me briefly and apologetically review the Church's Marian doctrines.

The **Immaculate Conception** and the **Assumption** are consistent with Luke:
- Hail, favored one!
- Most blessed are you among women.
- My soul proclaims the greatness of the Lord.
- From now on will all ages call me blessed.
- The Mighty One has done great things for me.

How can one read Luke 1-2 and not see that there was something very special and unique about Mary? I submit to you that the doctrines of the Immaculate Conception and the Assumption were consistent with the beliefs of the early Church. Given the last statement, you may be asking why the Church waited until the 19th-century (Immaculate Conception) and the 20th-century (Assumption) to declare these doctrines. I will address that question shortly.

Mother of God: If Jesus is God, why wouldn't Mary be the Mother of God? Why would the Church, in the fifth century, have to define this doctrine? Answer: The Church had to formally respond to the fifth-century Nestorians that argued that Mary was not the *Theotokos* (God-bearer) – but only the *Christokos* (Christ-bearer). The Church had to defend one of the basic truths of our faith – that the Word became flesh, died, and rose for our sins. The Church had to "bind" on earth this truth when it was under attack.

The Church waited until the fifth century to formally declare Mary the Mother of God – because that understanding was being questioned in the fifth century and the Church needed to firm up the truth of Mary's motherhood – for the Church and a world that needed to know the truth.

Reprise – the Immaculate Conception and the Assumption: So back to the question asked above. Why did the Church wait until the 19th and 20th centuries to define the doctrines of the Immaculate Conception and the Assumption? Mark Shea provides his insight:[90]

> *Darwin said the human person was an unusually clever piece of meat whose origins were as accidental as a pig's nose. Marx said humans were mere ingredients in a vast economic historical process. Laissez-faire capitalism saw people as natural resources to be exploited and thrown away when they lost their value. Eugenics said human dignity rested on "fitness." Much of Protestantism declared humans "totally depraved,"…. Freud announced that your illusion of human dignity was just a veil over fathomless depths of unconscious processes largely centering in the groin or emerging out of issues with Mom and Dad. …*
>
> *In short, as the 19th-century philosophies assaulted the dignity and **origin** of the human person, so the working out of those philosophies on the ground in the 20th century assaulted the dignity and **destiny** of the human person.*

*So what did the Holy Spirit do? Once again, in 1950, in the middle of a century that witnessed the biggest assault on the human person and on the family that the world has ever seen, the Church held up Mary as an icon of who we really are and who we are meant to become by promulgating the doctrine of the assumption of Mary. Just as the immaculate conception held Mary up as the icon of the divine dignity of **our origins**, so the Church … was now holding her up as the icon of the divine dignity of **our destiny**. …*

And that, in the end, is the point of Marian devotion and theology. Through Our Lady, we see Jesus Christ reflected in the eyes of His greatest saint.

Mary as Mediatrix: Mary, at the wedding in Cana, demonstrated her role as an intercessor between mankind and Jesus. She noted the wedding parties need, and she interceded for them. She became aware of a need and placed that need before Jesus. Sure, Jesus could have done all of this without Mary's intercession, but in fact, he hadn't; and (given the narrative) he probably wouldn't have. What did Jesus do? He honored Mary's request and performed the miracle.

"Taken up to heaven she did not lay aside this saving office but by her manifold intercession continues to bring us the gifts of eternal salvation. . . . Therefore the Blessed Virgin is invoked in the Church under the titles of Advocate, Helper, Benefactress, and Mediatrix" (CCC 969).

Mary's Perpetual Virginity: This is a topic where we can get all hung up on language and translation issues (e.g., brothers, cousins).

Note first the message that is conveyed in John 19:26-27. If Mary had other sons (who would take care of her per Jewish tradition), why would "the disciple" be introduced to his mother?

"This scene has been interpreted literally, of Jesus' concern for his mother; and symbolically…. Now that the hour has come, Mary ... is given a role as the mother of Christians (personified by the beloved disciple); …."[91]

But why a dogma about it? Because, again, Mary's life is a referred life. Her virginity, like Christ's, speaks of her total consecration to God and of our call as Christians to be totally consecrated as well. Her virginity is … a sign to the Church and of the Church. …

Jesus can do a world of wonderful things, but there is something even Jesus cannot do – He cannot model for us what it looks like to be a disciple of Jesus. Only a disciple of Jesus can do that. And the first and best model of the disciple of Jesus is the one who said and lived "Yes!" to God, …

This is why the Church, like the Gospels, has always called Mary our Mother: because Mom is the best model for training children.[92]

I addressed Revelation 11:19 - 12:2 earlier in Chapter 3 – *"The Ark" Prayer.*
I encourage you to meditate on the symbolism of this beautiful passage and what it tells us about Mary.

That's it in a nutshell – my brief apologetic perspective of the Marian doctrines and some of the biblical verses intertwined in those doctrines.

I am convinced that Mary is special. She was a favored one, blessed among women, and overshadowed by the Most High. The Catholic Church, then and now, calls her blessed and continues to look to her to proclaim the greatness of the Lord – to magnify the Lord.

As regards this book and from a Catholic perspective, Mary certainly is a "biblical biggie" – especially if we acknowledge "the fruit of her womb."

Catechism Check?

I believe that the prayer in this chapter is consistent with the *Catechism of the Catholic Church (CCC).*

I utilized the capability of the online *Catechism of the Catholic Church* (e.g., assumption, midiatrix) to locate the paragraphs cited throughout this chapter.

The paragraphs identified via **bold** numbers in the "Marian Doctrines" table provided, in my opinion, the best explanation of the associated doctrines. There are several other paragraphs that provide additional information on these doctrines.

It should be acknowledged that there are many other interpretations of what is conveyed in Revelation 11:19 - 12:2. The point-of-view noted in this chapter is my favorite, but I am in no way attempting to convey that it is the only valid perspective – nor the official position of the Church.

We Can Pray!

The Church, over the years, has embraced some beautiful prayers (e.g., *Hail Mary*, *Salve Regina*, *Magnificat*) that address the birth of Jesus and his mother.

As noted, Scripture tells us many beautiful things about Mary and her interaction with her son – from the manger to the cross. But in between not a lot is said about her and some of what is said almost seems derogatory. Mary is often on the outside looking in. This seems a little strange to us Catholics and leads some to question how blessed Mary really was – and is today.

"Her blessedness as mother of the Lord will be challenged by her son who describes true blessedness as 'hearing the word of God and observing it.'"[93] Scripture (Luke 2:33-35) hinted that this would occur and tells us why.

> *The child's father and mother were amazed at what was said about him; and Simeon blessed them and said to Mary his mother, "Behold, this child is destined for the fall and rise of many in Israel, and to be a sign that will be contradicted (and you yourself a sword will pierce) so that the thoughts of many hearts may be revealed."*

Mary's soul experienced the sword when Jesus lived. She experienced the sword at the cross. She experiences the sword today – so that the thoughts of many hearts may be revealed. Consider how the hearts of many have been revealed over the years because of Mary.

Some Protestants are very critical of the Church's doctrines regarding Mary, especially the Church's recognition of her as an advocate, helper, benefactress, and mediatrix. Many Protestants do not perceive Mary as blessed as we Catholics do and question why we pray to her and God – and not just to God.

The Church reminds us (CCC 435 and 487) that: "The name of Jesus is at the heart of Christian prayer. All liturgical prayers conclude with the words 'through our Lord Jesus Christ.' The *Hail Mary* reaches its high point in the words 'blessed is the fruit of thy womb, Jesus.' ... Many Christians, such as St. Joan of Arc, have died with the one word 'Jesus' on their lips. ... What the Catholic faith believes about Mary is based on what it believes about Christ, and what it teaches about Mary illumines in turn its faith in Christ."

We should constantly remind ourselves, and any who question our beliefs, of this fact. We can certainly pray that all come to understand this and at the same time recognize why all ages should call her blessed.

We can also pray that we come to fully understand what Jesus said to "the disciple" in John 19:27, "Behold, your mother." Have we taken Mary home as the disciple was instructed to do?

Around Easter 2004, Mel Gibson released the film *The Passion of the Christ*. As the anticipation for the movie built, there were a lot of concerns about the violence that would be depicted during the scourging and crucifixion scenes. I was personally wondering how I would react to those horrific scenes. I don't often break down and cry, but I tear up easily. When I first watched the movie, I got through all the violent scenes without much trouble – after all it was just a movie.

The scene that did get to me, however, was the flashback to Jesus the carpenter talking with his mother about a tall table that he was building outside. At the conclusion of that discussion, Mary, like a true mother, told Jesus to take off his dirty apron and wash his hands before eating. In a light moment, Jesus teased his mother by splashing some water on her; and then they shared a smile. That was the scene that filled my eyes with tears. That was the scene that got across to me the human side – the nativity side – of our savior and his mother.

We can certainly pray prayers of thanks to a God that provides such a savior, and a blessed mother who proclaims the greatness of the Lord.

Chapter 7

A Prayer of Thanks – for Saint Paul

Prayer	Vs.	Inspiration Verse
Father God, you designated St. Paul to know your will and to see and hear Jesus – the Righteous One.	A1	Acts 22:14-15
A light blinded St. Paul – on his journey – along the way.	A2	Acts 9:3-8
His companions also saw the light and led him by the hand for help.	A3	Acts 22:9
By your grace, St. Paul was what he was:	B1	1 Cor 15:10
He was the least of the apostles, not even fit to be called an apostle.	B2	1 Cor 15:9
But after he regained his sight, he was baptized, ate, and recovered his strength.	B3	Acts 9:18-19
While his eyes were still closed, he was told what he had to do:	C1	Acts 9:5-8
Get up now, and stand on your feet.	C2	Acts 26:16
Open their eyes – that they may turn from darkness to light. *Open their eyes – that they may turn from the power of Satan to God.* *Open their eyes – that they may obtain forgiveness and an inheritance.*	C3	Acts 26:17-18
By your grace, St. Paul was what he was:	D1	1 Cor 15:10
He was your chosen instrument. He carried your name before the Gentiles.	D2	Acts 9:15-16
He proclaimed Jesus in the synagogues as "the Son of God."	D3	Acts 9:20
He was your servant and witness.	D4	Acts 26:16
He would suffer for your name.	D5	Acts 9:15-16
By your grace, St. Paul was what he was:	E1	1 Cor 15:10
Breathing murderous threats against the disciples of the Lord, he started out to chain those who belonged to the Way.	E2	Acts 9:1-2
After he regained his sight and was filled with the Holy Spirit,	E3	Acts 9:17
he preached the faith he once tried to destroy.	E4	Gal 1:22-23
We thank you for St. Paul. We glorify you because of him.	E5	Gal 1:24
In you, we are his work.	E6	1 Cor 9:1

Background

After reading and discussing the first twelve chapters of Acts, including the Pentecost, my Bible study moved on to the remaining chapters (13-28) of Acts. The focus of Acts changes significantly after chapter 12, from St. Peter to St. Paul. St. Paul and his missionary travels became the primary focus of the last sixteen chapters of Acts.

Optional Challenge #2 at the end of the unit read: "Portray Paul in some art/prayer/literary form as you understand him from reading Acts."[94] The part of the challenge that most interested me was the phrase "as you understand him," since I have always had some difficulty understanding St. Paul.

So I took the challenge and wrote this chapter's prayer regarding St. Paul. As you may have already noticed, most of the prayer verses were inspired by verses from the book of Acts but I did stray from time to time to some of St. Paul's epistles that involved his conversion.

St. Paul was unlike the other apostles that we had studied in the gospels of Mark and Luke. Paul was not selected by Jesus to be his apostle – as Jesus traveled towards the cross at Calvary. Indeed, Paul (a.k.a. Saul) actively opposed the young Church that Jesus had founded – until Saul was converted on the road to Damascus. The story of St. Paul's conversion is told and retold in Acts (chapters 9, 22 and 26). Many of the prayer verses in this chapter were inspired by these three conversion accounts, which I will soon review.

We will also look at Paul the man and his interesting personality, before delving into the prayer. How did the other apostles and the Gentiles that he ministered to view him?

The Church's dogmas regarding faith, justification, and salvation have been heavily influenced by the writings of St. Paul. On the other hand, many of the theological divisions that exist between the Church and its separated brethren are related to theological interpretations of St. Paul's writings. I will touch upon some of those issues after I review the prayer – verse by verse.

But let me digress for the moment and ask you a question.

Question: Besides Jesus, name a religious figure you would like to ride across the country with in a car. ← STOP and THINK! Who would YOU pick?

Answers: Before considering the possible answers, let me explain the nature of the question. I was watching the television show *Family Feud* one evening about the same time that my Bible Study was reading Acts. During that episode, the question noted on the previous page was asked.

For those of you not familiar with this popular TV game show, 100 people are "surveyed" before each game and asked questions. The game contestants later try to guess what the top three, four, five or so responses were given by those who were surveyed. The more correct guesses, the more points and money the contestants – the families – win. One of the reasons that the show is popular is that those watching at home can also try to guess the correct (actually popular) responses.

To tell you the truth, I don't remember what name popped into my mind as my wife and I watched the show that evening. I also don't remember all the responses that "those surveyed" and the contestants had. I do remember that a lot of people chose Moses, which seemed like a logical response, especially if a lot of "those surveyed" were Jewish. As I remember, none of the popes were named but Mother Teresa, Buddha and the Dalai Lama were. Those surveyed were apparently a diverse group.

One of the responses could generate an interesting theological discussion. A fair number of the surveyed folks selected "God." I would have ruled that answer out, since Jesus was excluded in the question and Jesus is God (to me anyway). That is one of the fun aspects of the *Family Feud* – the answers that "those surveyed" give do not necessarily have to be theologically correct.

Anyway, after the question was read, my wife shouted out **"Paul!"** She apparently was one of the few that thought along those lines, as "those surveyed" had not named Paul or any of the other apostles for that matter – at least they were not named enough to make it to the top of the list.[95]

My wife's answer got me thinking. I was reading the chapters from Acts that described Paul in some detail and I was familiar with the biblical books (letters) that he had written. St. Paul certainly led an interesting life, and he had an interesting personality. He also left us some theological questions regarding justification and salvation.

The more that I thought about my wife's answer, the more I agreed with it. So, excluding God (invalid response?), I too would select St. Paul over Moses, Mother Teresa, Buddha, Confucious, Daniel, the Dalai Lama, Billy Graham, Peter, or any of the other popes. St. Paul would be my pick – assuming of course that I could work out the language and translation issues.

Some of the questions that I would ask during my cross-country ride with this missionary, apostle, and saint will be flushed out in the remainder of this chapter.

Paul (Saul) the Man

I find Paul to be one of the most difficult personalities in the New Testament to figure out. He was an emotional, all or nothing kind of guy – who seemed at times to me to be a little manic-depressive. (On second thought, maybe Mary, the Mother of God, would be a better companion on the car ride.)

Let's get a few of those basic biographical details out of the way first.[96] Saul was born around the year 10 AD. His father was a leather worker and a Roman citizen. Saul was raised in Tarsus, a city on the Mediterranean Sea in present day Turkey. Before his conversion Saul trained as a Pharisee in Jerusalem.

After his conversion (33-35 AD), Paul began his missionary work. He took three extensive missionary journeys throughout Greece and Asia Minor during his life, and he communicated with the communities that he visited via a series of letters. These letters, which have been incorporated into the canon of the Bible, tell us much about St. Paul's travels and life – but more importantly they tell us about the gospel that Paul preached.

Paul was a tentmaker by trade (Acts 18:3) but that work was incidental to his vocation as the "apostle to the Gentiles." Paul was arrested in Jerusalem around 56-57 AD and later escorted to Rome where he was executed around 62 AD. In a relatively short span of 52 years, he had lived an extraordinary life.

"The Acts of Thecla, a second century work, described him as a 'sturdy little balding bowlegged man, with meeting eyebrows and a somewhat hooked nose, full of grace. Sometimes he appeared like a man and sometimes he had the face of an angel.' We have no way of really knowing what he looked like, though there may be some merit in the description from Thecla."[97]

As to Paul's interactions with Jesus, we know:

- "It is all but certain that Paul came to Jerusalem after the death of Jesus and that he never saw Jesus during His earthly life; ... ."[98]

- Paul's first contact with Jesus most likely occurred on the road to Damascus. At that time Jesus spoke to Paul (per Acts 26:16).

- The gospel that Paul preached "came through a revelation of Jesus Christ" (Gal 1:11).

- The nature of the revelation noted above is unclear, except Paul apparently had some sort of mystical experience, as described in 2 Cor 12:1-10.

As to Paul, the preacher, and the apostle to the Gentiles; Luke (in Acts) and Paul (in his letters) provide us with most of the information we know about him.

Hopefully, I have provided you with some useful and valid information on St. Paul. I could continue to quote how others describe him, but I won't. Instead, I will provide you with my thoughts on St. Paul. While we were studying the letters that Paul wrote, we were asked two questions to draw out our thoughts regarding Paul. These two questions and my responses are noted below. My responses are not scholarly, but I think they adequately convey my thoughts regarding Paul.

Small group exercise after Acts:
"Luke gives his account of the Council in Jerusalem in Acts 15:1-21. Paul's remembrance of this meeting can be found in Galatians 2:1-10.
a) What differences do you find between these two accounts?
b) Why do these differences exist?"[99]

My response:

> *St. Paul seemed to be an "all or nothing" kind of guy – whether he was persecuting Christians or trying to save their souls. There were not a lot of grays in St. Paul's life – you were either with him or against him.*
>
> *St. Paul also seemed to have a big ego that was getting bigger as time went on. Regardless of what St. Peter may have done for the Gentiles initially, St. Paul seemed to want to assume credit for all the Gentile conversions – as he devoted his life specifically to the Gentiles – and as St. Peter devoted his life to the whole Church.*
>
> *I never sensed that St. Paul was particularly fond of the Jerusalem Church leadership (James and Peter). It wasn't too long after the Jerusalem meeting that St. Paul jettisoned Mark from his missionary team (Acts 15:38). Paul obviously would not hesitate to separate himself from those that he did not agree with or those he did not work well with.*
>
> *I think the Galatians account (Paul's account) reflects the above characteristics of St. Paul. The Acts account (Luke's account), on the other hand, was more polished and politically correct. The "we" and "us" entries in Acts lead me to believe that Luke knew of Paul's personality first-hand. Luke, much like a good presidential press secretary, may have presented a more bipartisan account of the meeting(s) in Acts 15.*

Assignment after studying 2 Corinthians: "Imagine you are a newly-baptized member of the Corinthian Christian community. Briefly describe your impressions of Paul as a pastor."[100]

My response:

Wow, the new pastor, Paul is something else!

Pastor Paul certainly is a complex person. To tell you the truth, I have trouble understanding him at times. He has so many phrases in his sentences that my mind gets lost as I listen to him. You certainly can not let your mind drift during his homilies. At times, he also seems very angry and a little paranoid to me. He has some close friends, like Timothy and Titus, but he seems to be fighting with many of the other brothers.

Pastor Paul doesn't have the "smoothness" that many pastors have. He doesn't have the stature, strong voice, or pastoral presence of some of the "superapostles" – that is what he likes to call the others who teach us. I guess what I like about him most is his fervor for the Lord.

If I could spend a day with Paul, I would ask him to be straight with me regarding salvation. Are those who say that all you need to do to be saved is to accept Jesus as your personal savior correct, or is there more? His message on salvation confuses me. I would also ask him to tell me more about his personal encounters with Jesus. Did he see Jesus on the road to Damascus or did Jesus come to Paul in a dream or trance? Last of all, I would ask him if he expected to go to Purgatory – or whatever you want to call it – because of the way he persecuted Christians when he was younger.

I don't think Pastor Paul will be at this parish very long. He seems to have itchy feet. He should be a missionary.

After the above assignment, our Bible study proceeded to study Galatians, Romans, Colossians, Ephesians, and Philemon. I learned much more about Paul, but my overall impressions (as noted above) did not change significantly. I obviously have some issues with Paul. I could certainly use a cross-country car ride and some one-on-one time with this great saint.

I will end this section with a couple of quotes from McKenzie that relate to Paul's strengths and weaknesses as a preacher and as an apostle.[101]

> *Paul often speaks warmly of his friends and companions, and there is no doubt of his friendly personality. One who spent most of his life meeting strangers and establishing close relationships with them must have been warm and outgoing. …*

> *His preference for statements which are extreme and absolute rather than qualified and tempered is characteristic of Semitic speech, not of Greek; and this habit has been responsible for the unfortunate fact that most heresies have based themselves upon the writings of Paul. One should notice also that none of the great movements of Christian thought have developed without a base in Paul.*

> *In him for the first time the Church and Jesus living in the Church encountered world civilization; and the Church has never learned a better language in which to address the world than the language of Paul.*

Jesus chose Paul to advance his message to the world and especially to the Gentiles. So just how did Jesus select Paul? How was a man who persecuted Jesus turned into such a fervent believer in Jesus? That conversion story is the topic of the next section in this chapter.

Paul's Conversion

The first account of Paul's conversion (**Acts 9**) is Luke's third-person account. Paul (or Saul, as he was known at the time) was briefly introduced in Acts 7:58, as a participant in the stoning of Stephen. His hostility towards the church in Jerusalem (Acts 8:1) and "the Way" (Acts 9:2) is interjected into the biblical narrative before the first conversion story is told in Acts 9:3-20.

The second account (**Acts 22**) is a first-person account – a speech that Paul gave to a riotous mob in Jerusalem that was determined to have him killed. That was probably a tough time to give a well-crafted and thoughtful speech.

The third account (**Acts 26**) is also a first-person account given by Paul, in what amounted to a trial in Ceasarea before King Agrippa and Festus – the Roman procurator of Judea. That was also probably a tough time to give a full and complete account.

Paul's Conversion (continued)

The fact that Luke repeats this testimony three times indicates that he believed it was very important. Likewise, since I believe the accounts are important, all three are printed in parallel on the following pages so that the similarities and differences in the accounts can be studied. You will see many of these verses again when we examine this chapter's prayer – verse by verse.

The three accounts are quite similar, especially as regards the details of what happened midday on the road to Damascus. Some of the words in the following accounts are **emboldened** to highlight some important similarities or some notable differences in the accounts.

The words of Jesus to Paul ("Saul, Saul, why are you persecuting me?") are identical in all three accounts. Those words apparently had a profound and lasting impact on Paul. The major differences in the accounts relate to Ananias' involvement in restoring Paul's vision in Acts 9 and 22 (but not in Acts 26).

Compare for yourself the three accounts. "All the accounts make clear the decisive importance of the Damascus experience not only in the conversion of Paul, but also in determining the personal qualities of his faith and his gospel: its focus on Jesus as the glorified Lord who has risen from His saving death and lives in His Church; ... The experience is difficult to analyze; there is scarcely any parallel instance in recorded history of such a sudden and complete personal reversal."[102]

Paul's Conversion Stories		
Acts 9	**Acts 22**	**Acts 26**
(3) *On his journey, as he was nearing Damascus, a **light from the sky** suddenly flashed around him.*	(6) *On that journey as I drew near to Damascus, about noon a great **light from the sky** suddenly shone around me.*	(12-13) *On one such occasion I was traveling to Damascus with the authorization and commission of the chief priests. At midday, along the way, O king, I saw a **light from the sky**, brighter than the sun, shining around me and my traveling companions.*
(4) *He fell to the ground and heard a voice saying to him, "**Saul, Saul, why are you persecuting me?**"*	(7) *I fell to the ground and heard a voice saying to me, "**Saul, Saul, why are you persecuting me?**"* **[Jesus includes a Greek proverb familiar to the Jews: If an ox resisted the stick used to prod him along, he would suffer more.]** →	(14) *We all fell to the ground and I heard a voice saying to me in Hebrew, "**Saul, Saul, why are you persecuting me?**"* *It is hard for you to kick against the goad."*

Paul's Conversion Stories (continued)		
Acts 9	**Acts 22**	**Acts 26**
(5) *He said, "Who are you, sir?" The reply came, "I am* **Jesus***, whom you are* **persecuting***.*	(8) *I replied, "Who are you, sir?" And he said to me, "I am* **Jesus the Nazorean** *whom you are* **persecuting***."*	(15) *And I said, "Who are you, sir?" And the Lord replied, "I am* **Jesus** *whom you are* **persecuting***.*
(6) *Now* **get up** *and go into the city and you will be told what you must do."*	(10) *I asked, "What shall I do, sir?" The Lord answered me,* **"Get up** *and go into Damascus, and there you will be told about everything appointed for you to do."*	(16) **Get up** *…*
		(16) *… now, and stand on your feet.* **I [Jesus] have appeared to you** *for this purpose, to appoint you as a servant and witness of what you have seen (of me) and* **what you will be shown.**
(7) *The men who were traveling with him stood speechless, for* **they heard the voice but could see no one.**	(9) *My companions* **saw the light but did not hear the voice** *of the one who spoke to me.*	← [Note: Acts 22:9 is out of order in this table] ← Why this disparity?
(8) *Saul got up from the ground, but when he opened his eyes* **he could see nothing***; so they led him by the hand and brought him to Damascus.*	(11) *Since* **I could see nothing** *because of the brightness of that light, I was led by hand by my companions and entered Damascus.*	**[There is no mention of Paul's blindness in this account** but note Paul's commission in verse 18 to remove the spiritual blindness of others.]
(9) *For three days he was unable to see, and he neither ate nor drank.*		
(10) *There was a disciple in Damascus named* **Ananias***, and the Lord said to him in a vision, "Ananias."* *He answered, "Here I am, Lord."*	(12) *A certain* **Ananias***, a devout observer of the law, and highly spoken of by all the Jews who lived there,*	**[There is no mention of Ananias in this account.]**

131

Paul's Conversion Stories (continued)		
Acts 9	**Acts 22**	**Acts 26**
(11) The Lord said to him, "Get up and go to the street called Straight and ask at the house of Judas for a man from Tarsus named Saul. He is there praying,		
(12) and (in a vision) he has seen a man named Ananias come in and lay (his) hands on him, that he may regain his sight."		
(13-14) But Ananias replied, "Lord, I have heard from many sources about this man, what evil things he has done to your holy ones in Jerusalem. And here he has authority from the chief priests to imprison all who call upon your name."		
(15) But the Lord said to him, "Go, for this man is a chosen instrument of mine to carry my name before **Gentiles***, kings, and Israelites,*		*(17) I shall deliver you from this people and from the* **Gentiles** *to whom I send you,*
(16) and I will show him what he will have to suffer for my name."	← → [Different emphasis]	*(18) to open their eyes that they may turn from darkness to light and from the power of Satan to God, so that they may obtain forgiveness of sins and an inheritance among those who have been consecrated by faith in me."*
(17) So Ananias went and entered the house; laying his hands on him, he said, **"Saul, my brother,** *the Lord has sent me, Jesus who appeared to you on the way by which you came, that you may* **regain your sight and be filled with the holy Spirit."**	*(13) came to me and stood there and said,* **"Saul, my brother,** *regain your sight."…*	

Paul's Conversion Stories (continued)		
Acts 9	**Acts 22**	**Acts 26**
(18) *Immediately things like scales fell from his eyes and* **he regained his sight**. *...*	(13) *... And at that very moment* **I regained my sight** *and saw him.*	
	(14-15) *Then he said, "The God of our ancestors designated you to know his will, to see the Righteous One, and to hear the sound of his voice; for you will be his witness before all to what you have seen and heard.*	
(18) *... He got up and was* **baptized**,	(16) *Now, why delay? Get up and have yourself* **baptized** *and your sins washed away, calling upon his name."*	
(19-20) *and when he had eaten, he recovered his strength. He stayed some days with the disciples in Damascus, and* **he began at once to proclaim Jesus** *in the synagogues, that he is the Son of God.*		
	(17-18) *After I had returned to Jerusalem and while I was praying in the temple,* **I fell into a trance and saw the Lord saying to me, "Hurry, leave Jerusalem at once**, *because they will not accept your testimony about me."*	

Note in the last verse above (Acts 22:17-18) the incentive that the Lord gave St. Paul to hit the road. If "they" (the Jews in Jerusalem) would not accept Paul's testimony, maybe the Gentiles would. The Gentiles were not otherwise specifically mentioned in Acts 22 (as they were in Acts 9:15 and Acts 26:17).

A Prayer of Thanks - for Saint Paul – How is it Structured?

Let's take a look at the prayer. How is it structured? What are some of the key components of the prayer?

I acknowledge that the title of the prayer is less than desirable. It is too long and flows poorly. Alas, I have been unable to come up with a better one. The title does convey the subject of the prayer – thanks (to God) – for giving us St. Paul. The prayer is not a prayer to St. Paul.

Overview

All the inspirational verses were selected from the conversion accounts that you have just read and several short passages that also alluded to Paul's conversion. They included: 1 Corinthians 9:1; 1 Corinthians 15:8-11; and Galatians 1:22-24.

This prayer is a mixture of "thanks" and "wisdom." Like the Psalms, this prayer contains many verses that acknowledge what God has done for us.

The prayer verses are arranged in the five sections described below:

Section A addresses "Father God" and then quickly proceeds with some "wisdom" verses. As we pray, we remind ourselves of what God has done for us through the life of St. Paul.

Sections B and **D** are similar in that they both thank God ("by your grace") for the work that Paul has done. The rest of these sections (wisdom verses) remind us of what Paul has done for us.

Section C provides nothing but wisdom verses – verses that specifically address how Jesus instructed Paul (blind at the time) to open the spiritual eyes of others.

Section E begins with thanks ("by your grace") and ends with thanks – to God – for St. Paul.

Verse by Verse

A1	Father God, you designated St. Paul to know your will and to see and hear Jesus – the Righteous One.

The first verse of the prayer is, for all practical purposes, a quote of the words that Ananias spoke to Saul as he restored Saul's sight. The changes made to the inspirational verse were made to clarify the names that Ananias used.

"God of our ancestors" was changed to **Father God** to begin the prayer – to direct the prayer to God the Father.

The "you" that Ananias was speaking to was **Paul** (a.k.a. Saul). Saul was the name used in Acts 7:58 to identify the young Jewish man present as Stephen was being stoned to death. Saul was the name used throughout the first conversion account in Acts 9. Acts 13:9 informs us, for the first time, that Saul was also known as Paul. "... there is no reason to believe that his name was changed from Saul to Paul upon conversion. The use of a double name, one Semitic (Saul), the other Greco-Roman (Paul), is well attested."[103]

The name of **Jesus** (the Righteous One) was also incorporated in the prayer.

Acts 22:14-15: Then [Ananias] said, "The God of our ancestors designated you to know his will, to see the Righteous One, and to hear the sound of his voice; for you will be his witness before all to what you have seen and heard."

A2	A light blinded St. Paul – on his journey – along the way.

The second prayer verse condenses the rather lengthy passage from Acts noted below. Note that Saul needed the help of others after he was blinded. Saul needed the help of others before he could help them.

The phrase **"along the way"** comes from Acts 26:13 – a parallel verse of Acts 9:3.

"*Christ provides for our growth*: to make us grow toward him, our head, he provides in his Body, the Church, the gifts and assistance by which we help one another **along the way** of salvation" (CCC 794).

Acts 9:3-8: On his journey, as he was nearing Damascus, a light from the sky suddenly flashed around him. He fell to the ground and heard a voice saying to him, "Saul, Saul, why are you persecuting me?" He said, "Who are you, sir?" The reply came, "I am Jesus, whom you are persecuting. Now get up and go into the city and you will be told what you must do." The men who were traveling with him stood speechless, for they heard the voice but could see no one. Saul got up from the ground, but when he opened his eyes he could see nothing; so they led him by the hand and brought him to Damascus.

A3	His companions also saw the light and led him by the hand for help.

Saul's companions provided him with the help he needed at the time. They knew that something significant had happened, but they did not no what it was. All they knew was that Saul needed help.

Compare the inspiration verse below with the account given in Acts 9:7, which has a very different account of what happened (*The men who were traveling with him stood speechless, for **they heard the voice** but could see no one*). Why the difference?

Irrelevant note: Your recollection of Paul's conversion (from past CCD stories, paintings, or movies) may involve Saul being pitched from a horse, when the light flashed in the sky. The horse (like the camels and livestock in the nativity accounts in Luke and Matthew) is not mentioned in any of the conversion accounts in Acts. Saul just "fell to the ground."

Acts 22:9 - My companions saw the light but **did not hear the voice** of the one who spoke to me.

B1	By your grace, St. Paul was what he was:

I don't normally repeat verses as I pray Scripture, but you will find this verse two other times (**D1** and **E1**) in this prayer.

This verse just reiterates – and reiterates – and reiterates – that all that Paul accomplished was by the grace of God. What is true for St. Paul is true for us.

1 Corinthians 15:10 - But by the grace of God I am what I am, and his grace to me has not been ineffective. Indeed, I have toiled harder than all of them; not I, however, but the grace of God (that is) with me.

B2	He was the least of the apostles, not even fit to be called an apostle.

The prayer verse above is not necessarily the view of this author. It represented Paul's belief regarding his own status – his role in salvation history (at that time).

"A persecutor may have appeared disqualified ... from apostleship, but in fact **God's grace had qualified him.**"[104]

1 Corinthians 15:9 - For I am the least of the apostles, not fit to be called an apostle, because I persecuted the church of God.

B3	But after he regained his sight, he was baptized, ate, and recovered his strength.

Note the importance of Baptism and the Eucharist.

It wasn't enough to be converted – to regain one's sight. Note that Paul did not recover his strength immediately. It was only after he was baptized and ate that he recovered his strength. This verse represents one more example of the grace that God provided Paul.

Acts 9:18-19: Immediately things like scales fell from his eyes and he regained his sight. He got up and **was baptized**, and when he had **eaten**, he **recovered his strength**. …

C1	While his eyes were still closed, he was told what he had to do:

This verse begins a section of the prayer that centers on blindness – both physical and spiritual.

From the wording of the inspirational verse, I conclude that when Saul asked the question, "Who are you Sir," he was blind (from the light) and/or his eyes were still closed. Paul was instantly aware of some "higher power" but he could not identify it. He was still the persecutor – spiritually blind to the saving power of Jesus.

Acts 9:5-8: [Saul] said, "Who are you, sir?" The reply came, "I am Jesus, whom you are persecuting. Now get up and go into the city and you will be told **what you must do**. … Saul got up from the ground, but **when he opened his eyes** he could see nothing; …

C2	*Get up now, and stand on your feet.*

The first step for Saul was to get up. Jesus had plans for Saul. Paul was to be his servant and witness. Paul had things to do. The first step, however, was simple (even for a blind man) – to just get up and stand on his feet.

This prayer verse and the one that follows are in italics to denote that they are pseudo-quotes of what Jesus said to Saul in Acts.

Acts 26:16 - [Jesus said:] "**Get up now, and stand on your feet.** I have appeared to you for this purpose, to appoint you as a servant and witness of what you have seen (of me) and what you will be shown."

C3	*Open their eyes – that they may turn from darkness to light.*
	Open their eyes – that they may turn from the power of Satan to God.
	Open their eyes – that they may obtain forgiveness and an inheritance.

This prayer verse emphasizes Paul's commission from Jesus – to "open their eyes." Jesus provides three reasons why this must be done – three reasons to open their eyes.

In Acts 26, there is no mention of Saul's blindness at the time but we are aware of Paul's blindness from the parallel accounts in Acts 9 and Acts 22. Isn't it interesting how Jesus challenges a man who had been blinded to open the eyes of others – to turn darkness to light?

Jesus provides us a sacrament to obtain forgiveness – along the way of salvation – to our inheritance.

Acts 26:17-18: [Jesus said:] "I shall deliver you from this people and from the Gentiles to whom I send you, to **open their eyes** that they may turn from darkness to light and from the power of Satan to God, so that they may obtain forgiveness of sins and an inheritance among those who have been consecrated by faith in me."

D1	**By your grace, St. Paul was what he was:**

There is that verse again. See **B1**.

This section of the prayer summarizes all that St. Paul did on Jesus' behalf.

1 Corinthians 15:10 - But by the grace of God I am what I am, and his grace to me has not been ineffective. Indeed, I have toiled harder than all of them; not I, however, but the grace of God (that is) with me.

D2	**He was your chosen instrument.**
	He carried your name before the Gentiles.

God specifically chose St. Paul. If you ever need an example of "the elect" think first of St. Paul. Note also that God had identified, from the start, St. Paul's role in salvation history.

Acts 9:15-16: But the Lord said to [Ananias], "Go, for this man is a chosen instrument of mine to carry my name before Gentiles, kings, and Israelites, and I will show him what he will have to suffer for my name."

D3	He proclaimed Jesus in the synagogues as "the Son of God."

Saul initially preached to the Jews in the synagogues. I love how McKenzie characterizes Paul in the following quote: "In his first preaching [in Damascus] he encountered the hatred of the Jews which pursued him the rest of his life; he was then what he has been since, the **great renegade**."[105]

Note Paul's profession from the start – that Jesus was the Son of God. Simon Peter had earlier confessed Jesus as "the Christ, the Son of the living God." From the beginning this acknowledgment of Christ's divine sonship would be the center of the apostolic faith (cf. CCC 442).

Acts 9:20 - and [Saul] began at once to proclaim Jesus in the synagogues, that he is the Son of God.

D4	He was your servant and witness.

Jesus, from the start, made Paul's purpose very clear. Paul was to serve Jesus. Paul was to be a witness to others. The inspirational verse below implies that Paul did not know everything about Jesus at this time. More would be shown to Paul later.

Acts 26:16: [Jesus said:] "Get up now, and stand on your feet. I have appeared to you for this purpose, to appoint you as a servant and witness of what you have seen (of me) and what you will be shown.

D5	He would suffer for your name.

Jesus, from the start, also made it clear to Paul that he would have to suffer. As you read Acts and the letters that Paul writes, you will see many examples of how Paul suffered. You will also note how Paul seemed to accept this fact from the start. He did not shirk this part of his assignment. At times he even seemed to embrace it.

Acts 9:15-16: But the Lord said to him, "Go, for this man is a chosen instrument of mine to carry my name before Gentiles, kings, and Israelites, and I will show him what **he will have to suffer for my name.**"

E1	By your grace, St. Paul was what he was:
There is that verse again. See **B1**. This section of the prayer summarizes the radical conversion that St. Paul experienced. The prayer will end with additional verses of thanksgiving and connect us with Paul's work for the Lord.	
1 Corinthians 15:10 - But by the grace of God I am what I am, and his grace to me has not been ineffective. Indeed, I have toiled harder than all of them; not I, however, but the grace of God (that is) with me.	

E2	Breathing murderous threats against the disciples of the Lord, he started out to chain those who belonged to the Way
The prayer verse above reminds us of what Saul was like before his radical conversion. The inspirational verse below begins the first of three accounts of Paul's conversion that I have previously noted. If Luke composed Acts between 80-90 AD, Paul had already been executed when the words below were written. Acts 9 was written to recount to the young Church – especially the Gentile Christians – how their apostle (the apostle to the Gentiles) was himself converted to **"the Way"** (a name used by the early Christian community for itself).	
Acts 9:1-2: Now Saul, still **breathing murderous threats against the disciples of the Lord**, went to the high priest and asked him for letters to the synagogues in Damascus, that, if he should find any men or women who belonged to **the Way**, he might bring them back to Jerusalem in **chains**.	

E3	After he regained his sight and was filled with the Holy Spirit,
This was the conversion – when Saul was filled with the Holy Spirit. In the prayer verse, I have chosen to capitalize "Holy Spirit," since St. Paul helped us understand the Trinity and the Holy Spirit.	
Acts 9:17 - So Ananias went and entered the house; laying his hands on him, he said, "Saul, my brother, the Lord has sent me, Jesus who appeared to you on the way by which you came, that you may **regain your sight and be filled with the holy Spirit**."	

E4	he preached the faith he once tried to destroy.
Think about the before and after diet pictures that you have seen over the years. Prayer verse **E2** = before; Prayer verse **E3** = the diet, Picture verse **E4** = after. The last three verses summarize the most radical change in the history of Christianity.	
Galatians 1:22-23: And I [Paul] was unknown personally to the churches of Judea that are in Christ; they only kept hearing that "the one who once was persecuting us is now preaching the faith he once tried to destroy."	

E5	We thank you for St. Paul. We glorify you because of him.
The prayer ends with thanks. Just like the Galatians, we glorify God because of the work that Paul did during his relatively brief missionary ministry.	
Galatians 1:24 - So they glorified God because of me.	

E6	In you, we are his work.
The last line of the inspirational verse is reordered. **In you** (in the Lord), **we are** (like the Corinthians) **his** (Paul's) **work.** This verse is linked to the prayer verse of thanksgiving above. "Looking over Paul's concept of the pastoral office, one is struck by the fact that it consists of two inextricably interconnected elements. • The first is that Christ called and appointed him as an apostle, by means of his vision of Christ on the road to Damascus. This objective factor relieves him of any dependence on the opinions and demands of the congregation. **'Am I not free? Am I not an apostle? Have I not seen Jesus our Lord?** … • But to prove that his calling as an apostle is authentic, he rests his case entirely on the second factor, his life, whose every aspect bears consistent witness that his claim is genuine. This is what makes him a lasting example to all who serve as priests."[106]	
1 Corinthians 9:1 - Am I [Paul] not free? Am I not an apostle? Have I not seen Jesus our Lord? Are you not my work in the Lord?	

Saints Peter and Paul

The two apostles that that have had the greatest impact on Christianity (with the possible exception of Judas Iscariot) were St. Peter and St. Paul. Their roles in the early years of the Church were documented in the Acts of the Apostles. Luke wrote extensively about St. Peter in chapters 1-8 and 10-12. St. Paul's conversion (Acts 9) and missionary journeys dominate the rest of Acts.

St. Peter was one of the first apostles – one of "the Twelve." He was present with Jesus during his earthly ministry. He was with Jesus during the good times and the bad. He was present at the transfiguration (Mt 17:1-9) and he was present in Jerusalem when Christ was crucified.

In contrast, **St. Paul** apparently never met Jesus during his earthly ministry. Acts refers to Paul as an apostle in Acts 14:14, only after apostolic ministry was expanded to include his missionary efforts. Saints Peter and Paul were contemporaries. They were the major figures in the early Church as it expanded from its Jewish roots to include the Gentiles.

So what did these two apostles think of one another?

Were they friends, brothers in Christ, and/or rivals?

Let me digress for a moment. At a business seminar that I once attended, the speaker noted that opposites were good – when it came to business leadership. The speaker's theory was that when the Chief Executive Officer (CEO) and Chief Operating Officer (COO) of a business had opposite personalities, the business was more likely to prosper and succeed over the long run.

If both the CEO and COO were gung-ho risk-takers obsessed with new ventures and long-term strategies; then day-to-day business decisions involving such things as cash flow, payrolls, and inventory levels suffered.

Likewise, when both the CEO and COO were conservative, risk adverse, and overly concerned about day-to-day business decisions; then things like business strategy and new product development suffered.

The best situation, even with its **inherent tension**, occurs when the two business leaders think differently. Over time, wise business leaders even come to understand, appreciate, and to some extent embrace the personality differences of their counterparts.

I tend to think of St. Peter as the conservative CEO, concentrating on the mission statement and policy. In contrast, I tend to think of St. Paul as a gung-ho (for Christ) risk-taker, continually striking out on new ventures, trying to grow market share. And like the wise business leaders noted above, I believe that Saints Peter and Paul came to appreciate each other.

I sensed from my study of Acts and the writings of Peter and Paul, that they were the opposites running the early Church – Catholic, Inc., if you prefer. They were certainly different. At times there appeared to be some **tension** between the two, especially Paul towards Peter. You can detect some of this tension in the two accounts of the "Council of Jerusalem" noted below. Compare the attitude in Paul's account in Galatians with Luke's third-person account in Acts.

> *[To the false brothers] we did not submit even for a moment, so that the truth of the gospel might remain intact for you. But from those who were reputed to be important (what they once were makes no difference to me; God shows no partiality) – those of repute made me add nothing. On the contrary, when they saw that I had been entrusted with the gospel to the uncircumcised, just as Peter to the circumcised, for the one who worked in Peter for an apostolate to the circumcised worked also in me for the Gentiles, and when they recognized the grace bestowed upon me, James and Kephas and John, who were reputed to be pillars, gave me and Barnabas their right hands in partnership, that we should go to the Gentiles and they to the circumcised.* – **St. Paul's account per Gal 2:5-9**

> *The apostles and the presbyters met together to see about this matter. After much debate had taken place, Peter got up and said to them, "My brothers, you are well aware that from early days God made his choice among you that through my mouth the Gentiles would hear the word of the gospel and believe. And God, who knows the heart, bore witness by granting them the holy Spirit just as he did us. He made no distinction between us and them, for by faith he purified their hearts. Why, then, are you now putting God to the test by placing on the shoulders of the disciples a yoke that neither our ancestors nor we have been able to bear? On the contrary, we believe that we are saved through the grace of the Lord Jesus, in the same way as they." The whole assembly fell silent, and they listened while Paul and Barnabas described the signs and wonders God had worked among the Gentiles through them.*
> **– Luke's view of St. Peter's leadership, per Acts 15:6-12**

I tend to read a lot of ego and sarcasm in Paul's account. Paul seemed to downplay the work of others with the Gentiles. In Acts, Peter pleads the case of the Gentiles. In Galatians, Paul limits Peter's mission to the circumcised. If I were Peter, I might have taken exception to Paul's account.

Others see Paul's choice of words as defensiveness (versus ego). They suspect that Paul was frequently challenged because he was not an eyewitness of Jesus' ministry. Paul had to repeatedly demonstrate that he also had been entrusted with the gospel (as Peter). Luke (in the middle) wants to emphasize the Holy Spirit uniting and guiding the Church. In Luke's account he acknowledges the debate first, and then the acceptance of the arguments made by Paul, Barnabas (and Peter). Even in the above accounts, where some **tension** is evident, you can see that Peter and Paul understood and appreciated each other's efforts.

Catholic, Inc. is over 2000 years old. There have been many divestitures and a few mergers over the centuries but, by almost anyone's standards, a 2000-year-old enterprise would be considered successful – a testament to its founder and the leaders that set the tone in those always difficult early years.

Saints Peter and Paul - Shared Beliefs and Gifts

1. Both Peter and Paul came to an early understanding that Jesus was the Christ, the son of the living God. It took Peter awhile to figure it out. Some help (revelation) from God the Father was required. Paul, on the other hand, obtained this knowledge almost instantly on the road to Damascus. Their acknowledgment of Christ's divine sonship was the center of the apostolic faith (cf. CCC 442).

2. Both Peter and Paul also shared the gift of healing. Peter (Acts 3:2-7) and Paul (Acts 14:8-10) each cured a crippled man.

3. As noted previously, both Peter and Paul agreed on the Church's approach to the Gentiles. Most Christians associate Paul with the Gentiles but the first fifteen chapters of Acts describe Peter's love and concern for the Gentiles.

Saints Peter and Paul Interact

Paul apparently did not interact with the other apostles to any extent. He almost prided himself on this fact – stressing that he received the gospel via Jesus (on or after the road to Damascus). Paul and Peter did, however, interact at least three times, per the information provided in Paul's letters.

The first interaction occurred more than three years after Paul's conversion, when Paul visited Peter (Kephas) in Jerusalem for a couple of weeks.

> *But when (God), who from my mother's womb had set me apart and called me through his grace, was pleased to reveal his Son to me, so that I might proclaim him to the Gentiles, I did not immediately consult flesh and blood, nor did I go up to Jerusalem to those who were apostles before me; rather, I went into Arabia and then returned to Damascus. **Then after three years, I went up to Jerusalem to confer with Kephas and remained with him for fifteen days.** – Gal 1:15-18*

144

Saints Peter and Paul Interact (continued)

The second interaction occurred fourteen or so years later when Paul journeyed to Jerusalem for the council meeting previously described. Paul presented the gospel that he preached to the Gentiles before the discussion with Peter and the others moved on to the question of circumcision for the Gentiles (as previously quoted from Acts 15:6-12 and Galatians 2:5-9).

> *Then after fourteen years I again went up to Jerusalem with Barnabas, taking Titus along also. I went up in accord with a revelation, and I presented to them the gospel that I preach to the Gentiles – but privately to those of repute – so that I might not be running, or have run, in vain.*
> *– Galatians 2:1-2*

The third interaction occurred sometime after the Council of Jerusalem, when Peter visited Paul in Antioch.

> *The decision reached in Jerusalem recognized the freedom of Gentile Christians from the Jewish law. But the problem of table fellowship between Jewish Christians, who possibly still kept kosher food regulations, and Gentile believers was not yet settled. When Kephas first came to the racially mixed community of Jewish and Gentile Christians in Antioch, he ate with non-Jews. Pressure from persons arriving later from Jerusalem caused him and Barnabas to draw back. Paul therefore publicly rebuked Peter's inconsistency toward the gospel.[107]*

In more contemporary wording, Paul chewed Peter out. Galatians does not tell us how Peter responded to Paul.

> ***And when Kephas came to Antioch, I opposed him to his face because he clearly was wrong.*** *For, until some people came from James, he used to eat with the Gentiles; but when they came, he began to draw back and separated himself, because he was afraid of the circumcised. And the rest of the Jews (also) acted hypocritically along with him, with the result that even Barnabas was carried away by their hypocrisy.* ***But when I saw that they were not on the right road in line with the truth of the gospel, I said to Kephas in front of all***, *"If you, though a Jew, are living like a Gentile and not like a Jew, how can you compel the Gentiles to live like Jews?" – Gal 2:11-14*

Paul mentions Peter (Kephas) a few other times in his first letter to the Corinthians (1:12; 3:22; 9:5 – Kephas had a Christian wife; and 15:5 – the resurrected Jesus appeared to Kephas). I will discuss the first two verses at the conclusion of this chapter.

Saints Peter and Paul Interact (continued)

Peter mentions Paul only once in his limited writings (i.e., 1 and 2 Peter).[108]

> *And consider the patience of our Lord as salvation, as **our beloved brother Paul**, according to the wisdom given to him, also wrote to you, speaking of these things as he does in all his letters. In them there are some things **hard to understand** that the ignorant and unstable distort to their own destruction, just as they do the other scriptures.*
> *– 2 Peter 3:15-16*

Note in the above citation from 2 Peter the positive references to "our beloved brother Paul." Peter (in 2 Peter) and Paul (in his letters) are saying the same things about God's will to save, the coming of Christ, and how to prepare for the judgment. Peter places the letters of Paul on the same level as the books of the Old Testament.[109]

Note also that even in the early days of the Church it was recognized that:
- some of what Paul spoke was hard to understand, and
- others ("the ignorant and unstable") are distorting what Paul said – just as they were distorting what was written in the other (Old Testament) scriptures.

Peter and Paul were different.
- Their interactions were few and far between.
- Their interactions with Jesus were different.
- Their personalities were different.

Like the great CEO/COO business leaders, however, they seemed to work well together and collectively they advanced the gospel. I will come back to Peter and Paul at the end of this chapter to discuss how their differences, shared beliefs and gifts impact the Church today.

The Gospel According to Paul

Paul preached the gospel but there are no gospels in the Bible that reflect his name. Paul's gospel was preached to his congregations and sprinkled amongst the letters that he wrote to them. Paul was proud of the gospel that he preached.

> *For I am not ashamed of the gospel. It is the power of God for the*
> *salvation of everyone who believes: for Jew first, and then Greek. For*
> *in it is revealed the righteousness of God from faith to faith; as it is written,*
> *"The one who is righteous by faith will live." – Romans 1:16-17*

After my Bible study finished Acts, we moved on to some of the letters written by St. Paul, specifically (and in the order studied): 1 and 2 Thessalonians, Philippians, 1 and 2 Corinthians, Galatians, Romans, Colossians, Ephesians, and Philemon. As we read and studied these letters, we heard Paul's gospel concerning faith, spiritual gifts, grace, justification, salvation, and the Church. It is in these letters or epistles (essays directed to the general public) that Paul's gospel comes to us.[110]

Thank God! Paul's letters have been an important resource for the Church as it developed its theology. Over the centuries, the Church has meshed Paul's gospel with other Scripture (both Old and New Testaments) and Tradition – "the teachings and practices handed down, whether in oral or written form, separately from but not independently of Scripture."[111]

Alas! Paul's letters have also caused great confusion and division over the years, especially when they are read in isolation (apart from other Scripture and Tradition).

Why? I will cite a few reasons why some of St. Paul's teachings have caused confusion and division. Note, as you read this, that the problem is not so much with St. Paul. It is with how we have utilized (and continue to utilize) the truths that Paul has passed on to us.

Firstly, cultural and speech differences account for some of the problems, as noted by Mckenzie. Paul would sometimes use extreme and absolute statements to get attention and then go on – and on – and on – to clarify those statements.

> *His preference for statements which are extreme and absolute rather*
> *than qualified and tempered is characteristic of Semitic speech, not of*
> *Greek; and this habit has been responsible for the unfortunate fact that*
> *most heresies have based themselves upon the writings of Paul.*[112]

Secondly, Paul's theology – his understanding of God – was developing as he preached and as he wrote. Take, for example, his beautiful imagery of the "body" (as it relates to "spiritual gifts" and the Church – as recorded in 1 Corinthians, Romans, and Ephesians). The imagery, as noted below, is consistent but you will also see theological development from book to book.

- The focus of **1 Corinthians 12** is "spiritual gifts." The first and last verses in this chapter use that term. The "many" gifts are compared to the "many" parts.

- **Romans 12** advances the topic using the imagery of the "body." Romans 12:4-5 is similar to 1 Corinthians 12:12, except Romans introduces the "function" of the body. Romans 12:6 offers a simple challenge, "Since we have gifts … let us exercise them." The chapter continues to exhort (offer, endure, persevere) us to use our spiritual gifts – like a Greek or Roman might exercise his body at the gymnasium.

- **Ephesians 4** advances the topic further by stressing the unity of the body through "him who is the head, Christ." The fourth chapter of Ephesians repeats "one" over and over to stress the unity desired in the body – in the Church. The "exercise" promoted in Romans 12 has worked – the holy ones can now build up "the body of Christ" (Ephesians 4:11-14).

Thirdly, Paul and others would often use the same words (e.g., faith, salvation) in two senses – sometimes more narrowly – sometimes more broadly.

> *In Romans and Galatians, for example, St. Paul uses "faith" broadly, to mean acceptance of God and his offer of salvation in Christ. This is the free choice of the will that saves us. But in Corinthians 13, St. Paul uses "faith" in a narrower sense in distinguishing faith from hope and love, and he says that love is greater. And St. James uses faith in a narrower sense when he says that faith alone does not save us. That is, intellectual belief alone does not save us.* [113]

Fourthly, Paul's presentations, to be frank, were not always clear. His sentences could be terribly long, filled with flowery phrases, and circuitous in format. Some of these clarity issues related to his use of words.

For example, his repeated references to the law (e.g., Galatians 3). The "sense" of salvation – as it related to the law – was not always clear. Was he speaking of natural law, the Old Law (the Law of Moses), the New Law (the Law of Christ), or some other form of law (e.g., civil)? Which "law," as regards our salvation, was he talking about?

Paul found it difficult to make clear statements. He sometimes spoke and wrote over the heads of his congregations. He seemed to forget at times that he was talking and writing to stupid people ("O stupid Galatians!" – Gal 3:1). If Paul could have distilled his flowery prose and lengthy sentences, he may have been able to come up with shorter doctrines that were more to the point, such as, "Listen you stupid Galatians: The New Law – the Law of Christ replaces the Old Law – the Law of Moses."

Mckenzie, in his entry on Galatians, notes that St. Paul may have been frustrated by his "clarity" problem. St. Paul may have recognized his insufficiency.

> [Galatians] does not have rigorous literary unity; it is bound by a unity of sentiment and psychological context. It is more deeply permeated with anger and emotion than any other letter, and it is the only letter which lacks the thanksgiving at the beginning and the final salutations (Wikenhauser). The conclusion [Galatians 6:11-18] was written in Paul's own hand; the depth of feeling and lack of schematic approach is shown by the way in which he repeats once more the urgings of the letter, **feeling that his point will never be sufficiently clear.**[114]

Lastly, Paul's writings cause confusion and division because of the way some Catholics (such as me) and other Christians "proof text" and "verse sling" his words. The following table contains a sample of verses that, to some extent, appear to be contradictory. Is faith all that is required? Are works necessary?

Romans 4:14 *For if those who adhere to the law are the heirs, faith is null and the promise is void.*	**Romans 3:31** *Are we then annulling the law by this faith? Of course not! On the contrary, we are supporting the law.*
Romans 10:4 *For Christ is the end of the law for the justification of everyone who has faith.*	**2 Corinthians 5:10** *For we must all appear before the judgment seat of Christ, so that each one may receive recompense, according to what he did in the body, whether good or evil.*
1 Thessalonians 5: 9 *For God did not destine us for wrath, but to gain salvation through our Lord Jesus Christ, who died for us, so that whether we are awake or asleep we may live together with him.*	**Philippians 2:12** *So then, my beloved, obedient as you have always been, not only when I am present but all the more now when I am absent, work out your salvation with fear and trembling.*

All the verses above tell us something about God's plan for our salvation, but they tell us more when they are combined into a coherent theology. When we "proof text" (use isolated verses to prove our point), we sometimes fail to communicate the totality of the gospel message. When we cavalierly abbreviate or modify verses to suit our personal point-of-view (e.g., a person is justified by faith **alone**), we fail to communicate the totality and truth of the gospel message.

Guilty? If you haven't noticed by now, "praying Scripture," as described in this book, is prone to "proof text" errors. Inspirational verses can be sliced and diced to a point where they can no longer be recognized. To a certain extent, this is a job hazard for anyone who uses Scripture to write about or pray to God.

The challenge, of course, is to maintain the truth of the verses cited, as they relate to the totality of the gospel message. That is one reason why each chapter in this book has a "*Catechism* check." It offers me an opportunity to go back and review what is written and assess whether God's truth has somehow been mangled. My goal for any prayer (and corresponding chapter) is to communicate God's truth. **Innocent?**

I hope that this chapter is not overly critical of St. Paul – the writer. Like all writers, he had his strengths and weaknesses. He certainly was prolific. His writings come across as sincere and they certainly reflect his fervor for the Lord and his mission to communicate the gospel to the Gentiles. As one of an elite group of best-selling authors, he certainly was successful.

Catechism Check?

I believe that the prayer in this chapter is consistent with the *Catechism of the Catholic Church (CCC)*.

This prayer was somewhat unique in that it dealt more with "personality" than "theology." The Church, rightfully so, does not waste a lot of space on "personality" – the *Catechism* is not *People* magazine.

This chapter contains my opinions and thoughts about St. Paul. This chapter reflects some of my problems understanding the totality of the gospel preached via St. Paul's letters.

I, like all Catholics, am blessed that the Church has incorporated the words of St. Paul into the entirety of God's gospel and the corresponding doctrines and dogmas of the Church.

I, like all Catholics, am blessed that the Church provides the *Catechism* to help me better understand the good news.

As to the prayer itself, it refers to Paul's characterization of himself as "the least of the apostles, not even fit to be called an apostle." Paul's humble assessment is not mine and it is certainly not that of the Church.

We Can Pray!

I noted a few pages back that Paul and Peter did not write about each other very often. They were more inclined to write about God. There were, however, two passages in 1 Corinthians where Paul mentioned Peter (Kephas) by name.

> For it has been reported to me about you, my brothers, by Chloe's people, that there are rivalries among you. I mean that each of you is saying, "I belong to **Paul**," or "I belong to Apollos," or "I belong to **Kephas**," or "I belong to Christ." Is Christ divided? Was Paul crucified for you? Or were you baptized in the name of Paul? – 1 Cor 1:11-13

> So let no one boast about human beings, for everything belongs to you, **Paul** or Apollos or **Kephas**, or the world or life or death, or the present or the future: **all** belong to you, and you to Christ, and Christ to God. – 1 Cor 3:21-23.

Even in Paul's day there were "rivalries" within the Church. Paul wisely tried to focus the attention of the Church on Christ, Christ's crucifixion, and our baptismal vows. Paul wisely noted that **"all"** (e.g., Paul, Apollos, and Kephas then; Peter, Paul, Mary, and John now) belong to the Church, the Church to Christ and Christ to God.

As regards this book on "biblical biggies," St. Paul reminds me in the passage above, "So let no one boast about human beings." They "all belong to you, and you to Christ, and Christ to God."

> No one questions [Paul's] position as the most creative thinker in the history of Christianity; indeed some have gone too far, asserting that historic Christianity is more Pauline than Christian. … In him for the first time the Church and Jesus living in the Church encountered world civilization; and the Church has never learned a better language in which to address the world than the language of Paul.[115]

Accordingly, we can pray – we can thank God for St. Paul.

Chapter 8

Does God Care?

The last chapter in each of the books in the *A Catholic Prays Scripture* series starts with the above question. It gives me (and you) an opportunity to reflect on the preceding chapters and think about whether God cares about any of the topics that I have written about. If you don't believe in God, you can skip this chapter.

In these closing chapters you will read a lot of questions concerning whether there are any right or wrong beliefs; and whether God cares.

- In some cases, I will throw in my two cents and tell you what I believe.

- In some cases, by context or reasoning, you will probably be able to figure out what I believe.

- In some cases, a question will be asked but not answered. After all, it really isn't important what I believe. It is important what you believe. It is even more important that you DO think about what you believe. It may impact your salvation.

Characters

This book concerned some of the 3,237 (or so) characters in the Bible. Some of them can be categorized as "biblical biggies," others as "bit players" in salvation history. We even discussed a few "villains," like the Pharaoh and Saul – a villain reformed on the road to Damascus – who became a saint.

Saints, Popes, and Doctors

St. Paul wasn't the only "saint" that we discussed. Our biblical cast of characters included St. Mary (the Mother of God), St. Peter (the first Pope), and St. Augustine (a great "Doctor of the Church").

"By *canonizing* some of the faithful, … by solemnly proclaiming that they practiced heroic virtue and lived in fidelity to God's grace, the Church recognizes the power of the Spirit of holiness within her and sustains the hope of believers by proposing the saints to them as models and intercessors" (CCC 828).

We sometimes unfairly place the saints on a high pedestal – at a level we can't reach. We should remember that one of the common characteristics of the saints is that they persevered. They overcome obstacles to serve God. They faced (and overcame) many of the same challenges that we face. Some of them even overcame themselves.

> [Jesus] turned and said to Peter, "Get behind me, Satan! You are an obstacle to me. … – Mt 16:23

Peter, an obstacle, became St. Peter. He was given the keys to the Kingdom. He became the Church's first pope. Likewise, Saul, an enemy of the early Christians, became the apostle to the gentiles. Augustine, an immoral youth, persevered and became St. Augustine and one of the great "Doctors of the Church."[116]

The Church teaches: "The witnesses who have preceded us into the kingdom, especially those whom the Church recognizes as saints, share in the living tradition of prayer by the example of their lives, the transmission of their writings, and their prayer today. … We can and should ask them to intercede for us and for the whole world" (CCC 2683).

Saints serve as models for us. I submit that their lives and their perseverance provide much for us to emulate – certainly more than many of the characters (e.g., actors, athletes, and musicians) in our lives that we tend to emulate. The Church celebrates the lives of the saints throughout the liturgical year, so that their lives and perseverance are always present for us to see and emulate.

"The patriarchs, prophets and certain other Old Testament figures have been and always will be honored as saints in all the Church's liturgical traditions" (CCC 61).

Many Protestants ignore the saints, except for some of the apostles. They even tend to ignore St. Mary – the Mother of God. They criticize or make fun of the Church's canonization process. They often question whether the "Communion of Saints" can intercede for us. Does God Care about what they think?

Biblical Characters and Theology

In the **Introduction**, I wrote about the four biblical images of the Church suggested by Hans Urs von Balthasar, which were based on four great New Testament figures: Peter, Paul, Mary, and John. These four images collectively support the Church, while at times creating a certain amount of **tension** within the Church.

I like to think of the Church as a radio tower beaming the good news to the world, with four tension wires – named Peter, Paul, Mary, and John – supporting the tower. In my analogy, tension is good. Without the tension of the wires – all four wires – the tower would collapse. Does God care which image we prefer?

In **Chapter 1 ("Abraham's Faith" Prayer),** I wrote about the immense faith of Abram/Abraham. God put Abraham to the test, and he was "ready." I also wrote about the theological connection between faith and works, a connection that has sparked Christian debate throughout the centuries. Are good "works" required of us or are they just a natural offshoot of our faith. From a personal perspective, I have never known anyone of great faith who didn't do (for whatever reason) good works. For me, the question of faith versus works is "a moot inquiry indeed."

Does God care if or why we do good works?

In **Chapter 2 (An "Exodus" Prayer)** I wrote about Moses (the great intermediary), a hardhearted Pharaoh, and the "exodus" experience of the Israelites. I wrote about dispositions of the heart: some negative (obstinacy and obdurateness) and some positive (*hesed* and mercy). God gave us a great gift and a great burden when he gave us "free will." We get to decide the disposition of our hearts.

Does God care how we exercise our free will?
Does God care whether we align our "free will" with his will?
Does God care if we are merciful to others?

In **Chapter 3 ("The Ark" Prayer),** I wrote about the Ark of the Covenant, where the commandments were placed. I also wrote about two aspects of how the Church views Scripture: the four senses of Scripture and typology.

Does God care if we observe the commandments – all of them?
Does God care if we try to squeeze every bit we can out of his "word," or would he prefer that we just stick to the "literal" sense?

In **Chapter 4 (A Tribute to Joshua),** I wrote about one of the great warriors of sacred history. In the chapter we also looked at some of the other warriors that have fought for God and his Church, including Pope Julius II, "the warrior pope." There continues to be a lot of evil in this world. There are still a lot of hardhearted people out there like the Pharaoh of old.

Has God called you to become a spiritual warrior?
Does God care if you accept his call?

In **Chapter 5 (Daniel's "Dream" Prayer)**, I wrote about Daniel, an unassuming biblical figure with an immense gift from God – the ability to interpret dreams. I also wrote about the dream of a Muslim man – a dream that caused him great hardship as he converted to Catholicism.

The Church (CCC 841) notes: *"The Church's relationship with the Muslims.* 'The plan of salvation also includes those who acknowledge the Creator, in the first place amongst whom are the Muslims; these profess to hold the faith of Abraham, and together with us they adore the one, merciful God, mankind's judge on the last day.'"

Does God – the God of Abraham – care about the way that his Muslim children are treated – when they study (theology) the life of Jesus?

Does the God of Abraham care about the way that Muslims act towards and/or are treated by Christians?

In **Chapter 6 (A Nativity Prayer)**, I wrote about the "Christmas" story – the nativity accounts in the gospels of Matthew and Luke. It is impossible for a Catholic to read the nativity accounts and ignore Mary, full of grace. In that chapter, I also discussed the Church's "Marian doctrines."

Does Jesus care how we view his mother?
Does God care how we treat his mother?
Does Jesus mind if we pray to her – to intercede for us?
Does God want us to pray to her – to intercede for us?
Does God care if you are only a Christmas (or Easter) Christian?

In **Chapter 7 (A Prayer of Thanks – for Saint Paul)**, I wrote about how Saul became St. Paul – the apostle to the gentiles – the greatest evangelist of all times. I also wrote about St. Peter and the tension that might have existed between these two great saints. I remind you again that in some cases tension is good (e.g., the tension wires holding up a tower, the tension between a CEO and his chief operating officer).

Is Christ divided?
If so, does God care?
If so, what should we do?

As to evangelization and apologia, Saint's Peter and Paul both understood Jesus' charge.

But the gospel must first be preached to all nations. – Mark 13:10

St. Peter, like St. Paul, understood the need for the church to spread the good news – the gospel – to anyone asking for hope, be they Jew or gentile then, or a Muslim man in Iraq today. If anyone is looking for an explanation, is looking for hope, we have the obligation to be ready. St. Peter – the rock instructs us:

> *Always be ready to give an explanation **[apologia]** to anyone who asks you for a reason for your hope, but do it with gentleness and reverence, keeping your conscience clear, so that, when you are maligned, those who defame your good conduct in Christ may themselves be put to shame. For it is better to suffer for doing good, if that be the will of God, than for doing evil. – 1 Peter 3:15b-17*

Does God care if we fail to explain our faith to those searching for hope?
Does God care if our knowledge of our faith is so poor that we can't explain it?
Does God care if we fail to preach the Gospel to all the nations?
Does God care if we fail to support our missionary churches?

Biblical Characters

In this book we discussed some biblical "biggies," some "stars" of Scripture. We have read about how some of the stars (e.g., Moses and Daniel) handled some of the villains in the Bible (e.g., the Pharaoh and Nebuchadnezzar). We have also read about some "bit" players like Uzzah and the magi.

To be very honest and upfront, you and I are probably "bit players" in the story of salvation history. Someone must play the lesser roles.

Thinking again about the cover photo on this book (as discussed on page 6); all those unidentifiable flowers, blades of grass, and weeds in the background collectively play an important role. Their roots intertwine in the soil and prevent the soil from being washed away. Without those roots, the hill, over time, would disappear. Over time, the chapel might collapse.

So remember that we also have an important role to play in salvation history. It is up to us to play our role to the fullest. It is our job to make the director proud.

Does God care about your character?

Appendix

Prayer Writing Techniques and Types of Prayers

This appendix is a condensed version of two chapters from my first book, *A Catholic Prays Scripture: and Tips for How You Can Too*. Those two chapters provided information on the techniques that I developed to pray Scripture; and the types of prayer that can be prayed.

This appendix is included for your convenience, as the prayer writing techniques and prayer type distinctions are also relevant in this book. For a more complete understanding of these topics please refer to the full chapters in my first book.

Part 1 – Prayer Writing Techniques

Five Steps to Pray Scripture

Listed below are five steps for praying Scripture. This appendix will provide more details on these five steps and some related computer tips.

Step	
1	Select Scripture, theme or "theology."
2	Read and meditate on the Scripture selected.
3	Select the verses that "speak" to your heart.
4	Incorporate the selected Scripture into a written prayer.
5	Be careful what you pray.

This appendix describes the process that evolved. It describes how I used a word processor and the Internet along with a few simple computer techniques (e.g., tables, "cut and paste") to write Scripture-based prayers. It should be noted, however, that these electronic tools are not required. All that is required is a Bible, some paper, a pen, some time, some insight, and (above all) a decision on your part to give it a try.

Throughout this appendix, computer tips (⌨) are provided. The tips reflect the electronic tools that I used. You may have access to alternative tools that work as well or better. If so, use those tools and your corresponding skills. If you don't have access to such tools and/or prefer to use paper and pen, proceed accordingly.

The five steps tend to flow from Step 1 to Step 5, but in actuality the steps are more fluid, more back and forth. You may find yourself going back every so often and hopefully thinking ahead a little bit as you *pray Scripture.*

Step 1 - Select Scripture, theme or "theology."

Note: Theology, as used herein, is meant to encompass some aspect (e.g., doctrine, tradition, rite) associated with the study of God and the Catholic Church.

Select a portion of Scripture (book and/or chapters), a theme, or a theology that you want to pray. The examples in my books will provide you with some ideas on how you can go about selecting Scripture to pray.

This step can be the most difficult step. Getting started is often the most difficult part of life. You should successfully complete this step before proceeding.

Step 2 - Read and meditate on the Scripture selected.

If, in Step 1, you selected a particular portion of Scripture (e.g., book, chapter, passage), all you must do is casually read over the text selected, as you would read a novel. Don't spend a lot of time at this point reading notes, commentaries, or other references. Just try to get a feel for the Scripture, the story being told, the style of the writing (e.g., history, wisdom, prophecy).

If, in Step 1, you selected a particular theme or theology, you must first locate the relevant Scripture to read. If you have some idea of the associated Scripture start there (e.g., baptism → gospel passages involving John the Baptist). Use a concordance or computer search to find verses related to your topic.

Most Bibles provide "notes" and/or "Scripture reference" information that can help you connect related Scripture references (e.g., a New Testament passage that may relate to an Old Testament prophecy).

There are many encyclopedias and dictionaries available to help you flush out the Scriptural passages that relate to a particular theme or theology. The Bible that I used had an *Encyclopedic Dictionary*, which was readily available as a reference. [117]

The *Catechism of the Catholic Church* has good indexes (by subject and verse) that can help one find the Scripture associated with a particular subject.

⌨ 1	All the prayers in this book were based on the Scripture found in the New American Bible. This translation can be accessed via the website maintained by the United States Conference of Catholic Bishops. http://www.usccb.org/bible/index.cfm [118]

⌨ 2	A Catholic Encyclopedia can be accessed online via the internet at http://www.newadvent.org. This encyclopedia provides more than 11,000 articles on Catholic topics.

⌨ 3	English translations of the *Catechism of the Catholic Church* can be accessed online at: • www.vatican.va/archive/ and • http://www.kofc.org/en/catechism/index.html To conduct a search of the *Catechism* on the Vatican website: 1. Go to: www.vatican.va/archive 2. Select "Catechism of the Catholic Church" 3. Select "English" 4. Select "Statistics and graphs" 5. Select "By first letter" 6. Select the desired letter (or number) 7. Scroll down to look for the word(s) that you want to search for. 8. The listing that appears provides a few of the words that precede and follow the "selected" word. These "phrases" provide some context for how the word was used. To obtain the complete *Catechism* paragraph for any of the entries, select the paragraph number (1-2865) on the left side of the screen.

⌨ 4	If you want to conduct a search of the New American Bible, I recommend: http://www.catholiccrossreference.com/bible/nab-search.cgi

Step 3 - Select the verses that "speak" to your heart.

After you finish reading and meditating on your Scripture selection, write out the verses that attract your attention – the verses that say something to you. The Scripture that you ultimately pray will come from the verses selected during this step. Don't overanalyze the verse at this point. If in doubt about a verse, write it down. Don't be concerned if you find yourself selecting a lot of verses. I typically selected three to five verses for every one that I eventually prayed.

- Look for verses that adore and praise the Lord. Such verses are useful for the opening and closing sections of the prayer.

- Look for verses that are poetic.

- Look for "prayer" verses. Many books of the Bible contain prayers.

- Look for verses that have unique or catchy wording.

- Look for verses that are repeated often. They are usually important.

- Let the Holy Spirit help you identify the Scripture to pray.

🖥 5	Instead of "writing out" the verses identified above, create a 3-column table using your computer's word processing software to capture the verses you select. An abbreviated example of this "capture" table is shown below. Rows can be added or deleted as appropriate.

🖥 6	Access an online Bible (per 🖥1 & 4) and cut and paste the verse(s) into the table created above. You might have to clean up the pasted verse a little and type in the verse numbers, but you will save a lot of time and minimize errors. I normally used [brackets] to clarify verses (e.g., Ex 9:16 below).

Example "Capture" Table:

[Then the LORD told Moses:] "... this is why I have spared you: to show you my power and to make my name resound throughout the earth!"	119	Ex 9:16
In your mercy you led the people you redeemed; in your strength you guided them to your holy dwelling.		Ex 15:13
The LORD spoke to Moses and said, "I have heard the grumbling of the Israelites. Tell them: In the evening twilight you shall eat flesh, and in the morning, you shall have your fill of bread, so that you may know that I, the LORD, am your God."		Ex 16: 11-12
... (additional rows as required to capture all selected verses)		. . .

Step 4 - Incorporate the selected Scripture into a written prayer.

The fun begins. Now is your chance to use your creativity to *pray Scripture*. Start writing the prayer from the verses you selected in Step 3.

I refer to the biblical verses that I incorporate into my prayers as *inspirational verses*. Something within these verses (e.g., the theology, the wording, a phrase, an action) inspired me. In some cases, all the words in the inspirational verses are quoted in my prayers. In other cases, the prayer verses are significantly different than their corresponding inspirational verses. If you review the *verse-by-verse* sections in Chapters 1-7, you will be able to see how the various prayer verses equate to or differ from the verses that inspired them.

The remainder of this section describes some tips on how to pray Scripture, but they are just that – tips. Use whatever techniques work for you. As noted before, I used a computer when I wrote my prayers, and the tips below reflect that process. If you are using paper and pen to *pray Scripture*, you may wish to consider using some note cards as you write and position your prayer verses.

🖥 **7**	Create a second 3-column table using your computer's word processing software to use as you write your prayer. I normally put this table at the front of the document that contained the "capture" table described in 🖥5. Cut and paste verses into this "prayer" table from the "capture" table as you build your prayer, per the suggestions below.

Nucleus - Go back over the selected verses. Usually one or two of them jump out. They can serve as the nucleus for your prayer. You can build on these verses.

A TRIP - Think about what kind of prayer you want to write. What mixture of **a**doration, **t**hanksgiving, **r**epentance, **i**ntercession, and **p**etition do you want to convey? What is the tone of the selected Scripture passages? Do you want to include any wisdom in your prayer or lament something that is bothering you?

Quote or modify? - Modify the verses that inspire you as required. As noted above, some prayer verses may be direct quotes from Scripture, but most are not. Don't be afraid to modify a verse to fit your prayer. Seek inspiration and use your creativity to write your prayer verses.

🖥 **8**	I suggest that you leave the verses in the "capture" table alone. Cut and paste from the "capture" table to the "prayer" table and then modify the verses in the "prayer" table as you wish. In this way, you will always be able to go back to the "capture" table if you want to start over or compare the final prayer verse with the verse that inspired it.

Person? - If your prayer is indeed your prayer, the prayer verses can be written from a "first person" perspective (e.g., *my* God, pray for *me*, *I* adore). In other cases you may wish to incorporate "we" and "our" into the prayer.

Layout - I usually divided my prayers into three or more sections, which I eventually labeled A, B, C, etc.

- Section A was the *introductory section*, my first opportunity to address, adore, and thank the Lord. Cut and paste the inspirational verses that you wish to consider for the introductory section of the prayer towards the top of the "prayer" table and then modify these verses as desired.

- I would also attempt to identify some verses that could make up the *closing section* of the prayer. Cut and paste the inspirational verses that you wish to consider for the closing section of the prayer towards the bottom of the "prayer" table and modify the verses as desired.

- The *body of the prayer* (B-?) by definition, is positioned between the introductory (A) and closing sections of the prayer. It helps to think of these middle sections as paragraphs. Each section, usually two to seven verses, should have a common thread. A section might contain the same types of prayer (e.g., A TRIP) or refer to a common person, place, or thing. The body of the prayer can consist of one or more sections. Refer to Chapters 1-7 for some examples of how I divided my prayers into sections.

9	When you go through the verses that you initially selected (i.e., in the "capture" table), consider using different colored fonts to identify the verses or portions of verses that you want to try to include in your prayer. This technique will help you pare down and/or categorize the Scripture.

Embrace Fluidity - The prayer is a blank sheet when you start. As noted above, my initial goal was to first find some introductory and closing verses and then fill in the body of the prayer. As I progressed the body of the prayer became cluttered with a lot of disjointed verses and incomplete sections. At such times, things may look hopeless. Don't give up! This is another time to seek inspiration and use your creativity. Feel free to move verses and sections around, to delete verses that don't seem to fit, to add some previously overlooked verses to complete a section, to re-modify a verse to make it read better. In short, *embrace fluidity*.

10	The "cut and paste" features of word processors make it very easy to move verses between and within tables. I used these features often to position the prayer verses within the prayer, as the sections of the prayer were refined.

Take a break - Sometimes it helps to take a break. Conditions are not always favorable for both inspiration and creativity. If you find yourself in such a situation, don't give up. Just set the prayer aside for awhile. I found such breaks, usually hours or days, to be very helpful. They were not always required but they were useful when I wrote some prayers.

Rewrite and rewrite until God's Scripture becomes your prayer. As you progress, the prayer will become tighter (e.g., fewer words, verses, and sections) and more structured. Keep making changes until you are comfortable with the prayer, as it relates to the Scripture that you selected. Rewrite and rewrite until God's Scripture becomes your prayer.

Identify Sections (Optional) - After the prayer is complete, I found it helpful to identify the sections. The section numbers become handy references (like biblical verse numbers) but more importantly they helped me ensure that the prayer was organized coherently and had some structure.

Example "Prayer" Table

A few pages back, I included an example of the "capture" table, which contained some examples of the verses that I started with as I wrote my first prayer. In actuality, the "capture" table had many more verses, most of which were never used in the prayer.

An example of the corresponding "prayer" table is shown below. It contains the prayer verses that were inspired by the cited "inspirational" verses. You can compare the two tables and see the types of changes that were made to the content and order of the verses in the final prayer.

Chapters 1-7 will give you the opportunity to make many such comparisons. As you look at the table below, remember that the verses were reworded and repositioned many times during the writing process. The table just reflects how the *finished* prayer was structured. Note the section (B) and verse numbers.

In your mercy, you led the people you redeemed. In your strength, you guided them to your holy dwelling.	B1	Ex 15:13
In the morning and evening twilight, you fed them.	B2	Ex 16:11-12
You spared them, showed them your power, and made your name resound throughout the earth.	B3	Ex 9:16

I used the word *finished* in the previous paragraph but since this is your prayer you can always change it to reflect your relationship with the Lord. In a sense, your prayers are never finished.

Step 5 - Be careful what you pray.

The last step of the process provides an opportunity to step back and think about the Scripture you prayed and what you learned as you prayed it. This step provides a time for reflection on three very important questions:

1. What did you learn from the process (of writing the prayer)?
2. Is the prayer consistent with the doctrines of the Church?
3. Do you really want to pray this prayer?

As to the first question, the process described herein requires you to read Scripture, to meditate on Scripture and (as a result) to hopefully learn from Scripture. Scripture tends to both answer and ask questions:

- What did you learn from the Scripture that you prayed?

- What did you learn about God (theology), about his Scripture, his Church (dogma and doctrines)?

- What did you learn about yourself?

As to the second question, you will note that Chapters 1-7 all have a section entitled "Catechism Check?" near the end of the chapter. In each of those sections I tried to assure myself that what I prayed was consistent with Catholic doctrine, or at least understand where it might not be.

"The *Catechism of the Catholic Church* ... is a statement of the Church's faith and of catholic doctrine, attested to or illumined by Sacred Scripture, the Apostolic Tradition, and the Church's Magisterium." [120]

11	The Vatican's official website (http//www.vatican.va) can be accessed to obtain a variety of official Church documents (e.g., encyclicals).

As to the last question, one should always be careful about what one prays for, as God may honor your request. More importantly, however, when (not if) God senses that you don't really want all your prayers answered, he may choose to dismiss all your prayers. What a terrible waste that would be.

Part 2 – "A TRIP" to Heaven "Plus"

The Five Purposes of Prayer

The *Catechism* lists the **five** "forms of prayer" that are noted in the left columns of the table below. Peter Kreeft, in his book *Catholic Christianity* notes that, "the Church's tradition, based on:
- her Jewish roots,
- the revealed examples of masters of prayer in Scripture, and
- two millennia of the wisdom of the saints,

gives us **five** themes or purposes of prayer [as listed in the right columns]." [121]

Catechism		Catholic Christianity by Kreeft	
Forms of Prayer	**CCC Paragraphs**	**Themes or Purposes of Prayer**	**Acronym (see below)**
Blessing and Adoration	2626 - 2628	Adoration (and Praise)	**A**
Thanksgiving	2637 - 2638	Thanksgiving	**T**
Praise	2639 - 2643	Repentance	**R**
Intercession	2634 - 2636	Intercession	**I**
Petition	2629 - 2633	Petition	**P**

The rest of this section will be organized along the themes identified by Kreeft, in part because he has identified an excellent way to think about and remember the five themes or purposes of prayer.

"A TRIP. Prayer is the greatest of all trips we can take: a trip to heaven."[122]

I prefer Kreeft's **"A TRIP"** organization (versus the *Catechisms*) for two other reasons:

1. I have trouble distinguishing between "adoration" and "praise."

2. While I recognize that many people petition God for forgiveness, I know that there are many worldly reasons that people petition God (e.g., for health, for love, for money). Since "repentance" is more spiritual in nature (i.e., between God and man), I believe it deserves to be separated out from "petition."

The scriptural prayers described in this book utilize a mixture of these themes. Most of the prayers start and end with **a**doration. In between are prayers of **t**hanksgiving, **r**epentance, **i**ntercession, and **p**etition.

Adoration and Praise

The *Catechism* (CCC 2628) states that, "*Adoration* is the first attitude of man **acknowledging** that he is a creature before his Creator. It exalts the greatness of the Lord who made us and the almighty power of the Savior who sets us free from evil."

"Praise is the form of prayer which recognizes most immediately that God is God. It lauds God for his own sake and gives him glory, quite beyond what he does, but simply because **HE IS**" (CCC 2639).

The Old Testament, especially the books of the Pentateuch (e.g., Exodus 3), describes God. How good it is that we can use Scripture and prayer to acknowledge these words and adore God. We acknowledge, adore and praise God because **HE deserves it**.

Thanksgiving

Giving thanks is a very common action for most people today. We are forever thanking the people we encounter each day, usually for the little things that they do for us, indeed even for the little things that they are often paid to do for us.

We are not always as good about thanking God for the marvelous things that he freely does for us each day, from that first conscience breath in the morning to the last one before we return to sleep.

In John 11:41-42, we hear Jesus say, "Father, I thank you for hearing me. **I know that you always hear me**." What better example of a "thanksgiving prayer" do we need? What better reason do we need to thank the Father?

Every event in our life can be an occasion for thanks, even those events that are not as pleasant as our human nature would prefer.

Saint Paul, in 1 Thessalonians 5:16-18, tells us to, "Rejoice always. Pray without ceasing. In all circumstances give thanks, for this is the will of God for you in Christ Jesus."

Repentance

The *Catechism* treats "repentance" as the first movement of a prayer of petition. Kreeft, in his book, separates "repentance" from petition and treats it as a stand-alone theme or purpose of prayer.[123] Irrespective of this difference, repentance is the same.

The *Catechism* states that: "The first movement of the prayer of petition is *asking forgiveness*, like the tax collector in the parable: 'God, be merciful to me a sinner!' It is a prerequisite for righteous and pure prayer" (CCC 2631).

We cannot righteously pray to God if we have not repented for our sins. We should not expect God to honor our prayers of petitions if they are not pure. As we *pray Scripture,* we should be on the look out for those who are honestly repenting for their sins. You will most likely also note how their petitions are often granted.

Intercession

Intercession is a special type of prayer of petition, whereby we ask for something on behalf of another.

Scripture provides us with many good examples of intercessors.

- "Since Abraham, intercession – asking on behalf of another – has been characteristic of a heart attuned to God's mercy" (CCC 2635).

- Moses provided some of the most striking examples of intercessory prayer (cf. CCC 2574). His intercession on behalf of his people was nothing short of heroic.

- The Apostle Paul interceded on behalf of his Christian communities. "The first Christian communities lived this form of fellowship intensely" (CCC 2636).

- "[Jesus] is the one intercessor with the Father on behalf of all men, especially sinners" (CCC 2634).

Our intercessions should be boundless: for our families, for our friends, for our neighbors, for those who reject the Scripture that we pray, and even for those who persecute us.

Petition

"Man is a beggar before God." [124]

"The vocabulary of supplication in the New Testament is rich in shades of meaning: ask, beseech, plead, invoke, entreat, cry out, even 'struggle in prayer.' Its most usual form ... is petition ..." (CCC 2629).

Prayers of petitions are often cries for help, but they are cries buoyed by hope in the risen Christ (cf. CCC 2630).

We note in Mark 11:24 that Jesus said, "... all that you ask for in prayer, believe that you will receive it and it shall be yours." We also note from Matthew 6:9-10 that Jesus said, "Our Father in heaven ... your will be done, on earth as in heaven." Our petitions to God should recognize and reflect this paradox.

Scripture abounds with prayers of petition. As you *pray Scripture*, look at and learn from the petitions that are granted.

Two Other Forms of Prayer – This is the "Plus" Part

I submit that there are two other forms of prayer that can be found in Scripture (in addition to **A TRIP**). These other forms of "implied" prayer are particularly evident in Psalms.

Laments are typically variations of a "Woe is me, because ..." statement, where the "because" describes the various trials that the writer is experiencing. If someone says, "Woe is me, because ..." they are asking for help. The implied prayer is: "Lord, help me accept my woe and/or help me resolve it." Laments are implied petitions.

Wisdom is often expressed in simple statements of fact (e.g., Psalm 3:9 – "Safety comes from the Lord!") or as instructions (e.g., Psalm 95:8 – "Do not harden your hearts"). The implied prayer is that the person hearing the wisdom thanks God for the knowledge, instructions, or advice provided.

Praying Scripture – As Described Herein

While Scripture contains some wonderful prayers, not all Scripture is prayer. This book, via the techniques described in this appendix and the example prayers, can help you pray those Scripture passages that don't normally prompt prayer.

Anyone who has ever taught knows that you learn more by teaching than your students do by listening. The teacher learns by preparing.

Praying Scripture is very similar:
You learn about God as you turn Scripture into prayer.
You take in what God wants to tell you.
You meditate over it.
You digest it.
You reformulate it and then you use it to:

- adore God,
- thank God,
- repent,
- ask for intercession or
- petition God.

You go on A TRIP to heaven!

Let God hear your laments, so that he can help you.

Let wisdom statements and instructions engender thanksgiving and encourage adoration.

Endnotes and Amplifications

Introduction

[1]   Cf: https://www.wordsearchbible.com/products/28596. This website attributes the *Biographical Bible* by David G. Stephan as the source of the answer.

[2]   George Weigel, "Mary was beginning of discipleship," *The Catholic Voice* (the Archdiocese of Omaha newspaper), May 23, 2003, 22. The **emphasis** is mine and the quote was modified slightly to reflect the order change from: Paul, John, Peter and Mary.

[3]   Details from the NAB account from 1 Samuel 30:1 through 2 Samuel 1:27, plus details from 1 Samuel 18:11 ("nail"), 19:10 ("nail"), and 27:6 ("Achish). Geographic details on the location of Ziklag and Mt. Gilboa from McKenzie's *Dictionary of the Bible* and Hammond's *Atlas of the Bible Lands*.

Chapter 1: "Abraham's Faith" Prayer

[4]   *New American Bible* note concerning Daniel 3:24-90. "These verses are inspired additions to the Aramaic text of Daniel, translated from the Greek form of the book. They were originally composed in Hebrew or Aramaic, which has not been preserved. The church has always regarded them as part of canonical Scriptures."

[5]   John L. McKenzie, S.J., *Dictionary of the Bible* (New York: Touchstone, 1995 Edition), "Azariah" on page 71.

[6]   *New American Bible* note concerning Genesis 14:18.

[7]   *New American Bible* note concerning Genesis 14:19.

[8]   *New American Bible* note concerning Genesis 14:20.

[9]   James Akin, *The Salvation Controversy* (San Diego: Catholic Answers, 2001).

[10] Akin, *The Salvation Controversy,* Chapter 8, pages 94-122.

[11] Akin, *The Salvation Controversy,* 119.

[12] Akin, *The Salvation Controversy,* 121.

Chapter 2: An "Exodus" Prayer

[13] Archdiocese of Denver, *Old Testament Foundations: Genesis Through Kings: Year One Student Workbook* (Mahwah, NJ: Paulist Press, 1994), 8.

[14] John L. McKenzie, S.J., *Dictionary of the Bible* (New York: Touchdown, 1995 Edition), 588-589 "Moses."

[15] Cf. 257 "Exodus."

[16] 588 "Moses" ("plaster saint" phrase).

[17] 516 "Lord."

[18]   NAB note to Romans 9:14-18.

[19]   Cf. NAB notes to Nm 20:11 and 12f. In a similar situation described in Ex 17:6, Moses only struck the rock once. In Nm 20:24, the Lord reiterated his reasoning ("because you rebelled against my commandment at the waters of Meribah"). The NAB note to Nm 20:12f suggests that the "sin of Moses and Aaron consisted in doubting God's mercy toward the ever-rebellious people." Some scholars also speculate that Moses' fault was that he didn't show forth the Lord's sanctity by noting that their location at the time (Kadesh) meant "sanctified, sacred."

[20]   McKenzie, 566-567 "Mercy."
        The entire section of the chapter regarding *hesed* was Cf. pages 565-567.

[21]   The New Testament use of the Greek word *eleos*, which is often rendered mercy, reflects the revolutionary development of love by Jesus, St. Paul, and others in the New Testament. As such, *eleos* becomes the duty of one man to another (with less concern for position or rank). This duty requires a readiness to forgive and the performance of good deeds. The *eleos* of God also appears more frequently as the will to save (Cf. McKenzie, 567 "Mercy").

[22]   NAB note to Romans 9:14-18.

[23]   NAB note to Romans 9:18.

[24]   NAB note to Romans 9:19-29.

[25]   *The New Advent Catholic Encyclopedia* (www.newadvent.org/cathen/03477c.htm) online article on "Pope St. Celestine I."

[26]   Cf. Chapters 43 and 45 of Aurelius Augustine's *A treatise on Grace and Free Will,* 426 or 427 A.D. I took the liberty of "Americanizing the quotes. The original translation can be found online at http://www.newadvent.org/fathers/1510.htm.

[27]   Reverend Peter M. J. Stravinskas, *Our Sunday Visitor's Catholic Encyclopedia* (Huntington, Indiana: Our Sunday Visitor, 1998 Edition), Cf. encyclopedia entries on "Doctor," "Fathers of the Church (also Apostolic Fathers," and "Tradition."

Chapter 3: "The Ark" Prayer

[28]   Archdiocese of Denver, *Old Testament Foundations: Genesis Through Kings: Year One Student Workbook* (Mahwah, NJ: Paulist Press, 1994), 12.

[29]   http://www.bible-history.com/art/tabrncl.htm
        Photo Credit: Artwork by Priscilla Silver, Graphic Design by Rusty Russell.

[30]   Henry G. Graham, *Where We Got the Bible* (San Diego: Catholic Answers, 1997), 58-59.

[31]   St. Augustine, *De serm. Dom. in monte* (as cited in CCC 2794).

[32]   CCC 1257, **emphasis** (but not *Italics*) added. This is a wonderful statement for us judgmental folks to remember. God is not bound by his sacraments – he will show mercy to and take pity on whom he wants to (cf. Romans 9:14-18).

[33] Anagogy comes from a Greek word meaning "leading up." Thus, scripture can lead us up (to heaven). The word anagogy, itself, is defined as a "mystical interpretation."

[34] Examples 1 and 2 were developed from a Bible study handout concerning "the senses of scripture." Example 3 developed, in part, from the Hahn book (*Hail, Holy Queen*) cited below. It should be acknowledged that the spiritual senses of Scripture are based on the literal, and it is the task of the exegetes to help the Church understand and explain Scripture. Scripture is ultimately subject to the judgment of the Church (cf. CCC 119).

[35] New York: Doubleday, 2001.

[36] Scott Hahn, *Hail, Holy Queen: The Mother of God in the Word of God.* (New York: Doubleday, 2001). Chapter 3 (pages 49 – 67). The four quotes were from pages 55, 60, 60-61, and 61.

[37] The online *Catechism* maintained by the Knights of Columbus. See the appendix for additional details.

Chapter 4: A Tribute to Joshua

[38] Cf. New American Bible note concerning Nm 13:16.

[39] Cf. New American Bible note concerning Jos 10:13.

[40] For a biblical cookbook, go to http://www.cookingwiththebible.com/.

[41] Bernhard W. Anderson, *Understanding the Old Testament*, Second Edition (Englewood Cliffs, New Jersey: Prentice Hall, 1966), 18.

[42] 19, bold font mine.

[43] 1-2, bold font mine.

[44] 2.

[45] 93.

[46] 48-49, bold font mine.

[47] Peter Kreeft, *You Can Understand the Old Testament* (Ann Arbor, Michigan: Servant Publications, 1990), 52-53.

[48] John L. McKenzie, *Dictionary of the Bible* (New York: Simon & Schuster, First Touchstone Edition, 1995), "Type, typology" on pages 903-904.

[49] Cf. 904.

[50] Kreeft, 54 (also cf. the table below the quote).

[51] McKenzie, "Joshua" on page 457.

Chapter 5: Daniel's "Dream" Prayer

[52]   Peter Kreeft, *You Can Understand the Old Testament* (Ann Arbor, Michigan: Servant Publications, 1990), 149, bold font mine.

[53]   John L. McKenzie, *Dictionary of the Bible* (New York: Simon & Schuster, First Touchstone Edition, 1995), "Daniel" on pages 172, bold font mine.

[54]   Toni Craven, *Collegeville Bible Commentary: Ezekiel, Daniel* (Collegeville, Minnesota: The Liturgical Press, 1986), 102.

[55]   121.

[56]   New American Bible note concerning Ez 14:14.

[57]   Bernhard W. Anderson, *Understanding the Old Testament*, Second Edition (Englewood Cliffs, New Jersey: Prentice-Hall, 1966), 537.

[58]   New American Bible note concerning Dn 4:10.

[59]   Craven, 6 (bold font mine).

[60]   Kreeft, 149.

[61]   Cf. Craven. (Section titles from pages 103 – 139).

[62]   McKenzie, (Cf. and quotes in this column from pages 172 – 174).

[63]   Cf. New American Bible note concerning Dn 8:9.

[64]   Craven, 126.

[65]   134.

[66]   Anderson, 536 (bold font mine).

[67]   Will Durant, *The Life of Greece* (New York: Simon and Schuster, 1939 – renewed 1966).

[68]   573-574 (my paragraphs and bold fonts).

[69]   579-582 (my paragraphs, bullets, and bold fonts).

[70]   603-606 (my paragraphs and bold fonts).

[71]   Wikipedia "Dream" on 4-08-14.

[72]   Joseph Fadelle, *The Price to Pay: A Muslim Risks All to Follow Christ* (San Francisco: Ignatius Press, 2012), 34 (bold fonts mine).

[73]   35 (bold fonts mine, two paragraphs combined into one).

[74]   36 (two paragraphs combined into one).

[75]   72-73 (bold fonts mine, paragraphs combined).

Chapter 6: A Nativity Prayer

76   Archdiocese of Denver, *New Testament Foundations: Jesus and Discipleship: Year Two Student Workbook.* (Mahwah, NJ: Paulist Press, 1995), 12.

77   Merrill C. Tenney, *New Testament Survey,* Revised by Walter M. Dunnett (Grand Rapids, Michigan: Wm. B. Eerdmans Publishing Co., 1985), Cf. 149-187. Most of the information in the table was obtained from this source. On page 161 there are some comments concerning the disagreement between Mark and Paul that is described in Acts 11-15.

78   Macrina Scott, O.S.F., "How to Read the Nativity Stories of Jesus," as included (supplemental reading) in *New Testament Foundations: Jesus and Discipleship,* Cf. 77-81 for this table and the next.

79   John L. McKenzie, *Dictionary of the Bible* (New York: Simon & Schuster, First Touchstone Edition, 1995), Cf. "Emmanuel" on pages 234-235.

80   McKenzie, *Dictionary of the Bible*, Cf. "Magi" on page 534.

81   Cf. New American Bible note concerning Lk 1.5 - 2.52.

82   Cf. New American Bible note concerning Mt 1.1 - 2.23.

83   Cf. New American Bible note concerning Mt 2.23.

84   New American Bible note concerning Mt 1.1 - 2.23 (my **emphasis**).

85   *Ineffabilis Deus* (Denz. 1641) as quoted in Keating (see below), 269-270.

86   *Munificentissimus Deus* (Denz. 2333) as quoted in Keating (see below), 273.

87   Cf. *Lumen Gentium* paragraph 62 (available at the www.vatican.va website).

88   St. Augustine, *Serm.* 186, 1: PL38, 999, as quoted in CCC 510.

89   Karl Keating, *Catholicism and Fundamentalism, The Attack of "Romanism" by "Bible Christians"* (San Francisco: Ignatius Press, 1988), 268-289.

90   Mark P. Shea, "The Mother of the Son: The Case for Marian Devotion," *Crisis*, December 2004: 20. Mr. Shea's quotes were abbreviated (...) and rearranged. **Emphasis** is mine.

91   New American Bible note concerning John 19:26-27. The NAB note provided several other suggestions concerning how John 19:27 - 20:2 could be understood.

92   Shea, "The Mother of the Son...", 19.

93   New American Bible note concerning Lk 2:35.

Chapter 7: A Prayer of Thanks – for St. Paul

94   Archdiocese of Denver, *New Testament Foundations: Jesus and Discipleship: Year Two Student Workbook* (Mahwah, NJ: Paulist Press, 1995), 24.

95   The question was asked during the 2003-2004 *Family Feud* season. I recently was able to verify the question via the intranet (http://mstiescott.tripod.com/feud5.html). My memory had mangled the question some. The correct question, per the website, was asked in this chapter. My memory regarding the survey responses was pretty good. The actual responses, per the website, were: Moses (26), God (15), Buddha (14), Mary Magdalene (8), Dahlia Lama (7), and Mother Teresa (7). The other 23 people surveyed had less "popular" (six or less) responses.

96   *Our Sunday Visitor's Catholic Encyclopedia* (Huntington, IN: Our Sunday Visitor Publishing Division, 1998 revised edition), cf. "Paul, St." on page 763.

97   Alfred McBride, O. Praem., *The Gospel of the Holy Spirit: Meditation and Commentary on the Acts of the Apostles* (Huntington, IN: Our Sunday Visitor Publishing Division, 1992), 91.

98   John L. McKenzie, *Dictionary of the Bible* (New York: Simon & Schuster, First Touchstone Edition, 1995), "Paul" on page 648.

99   *New Testament Foundations*, 24.

100   *New Testament Foundations*, 30.

101   McKenzie, *Dictionary of the Bible*, 650-651.

102   McKenzie, *Dictionary of the Bible*, 648-649.

103   New American Bible note regarding Acts 13:9.

104   New American Bible note regarding 1 Cor 15:9-11.

105   McKenzie, *Dictionary of the Bible*, 649.

106   Hans Urs von Balthaser, *Paul Struggles with His Congregation: The Pastoral Message of the Letters to the Corinthians* (San Francisco: Ignatius, 1992), as translated by Brigitte L. Bojarska, bullets and **emphasis** are mine, 36.

107   New American Bible note regarding Galatians 2:11-14 (verse references removed).

108   The author of 2 Peter, like many books in the Bible, is disputed by some. As such, it is recognized that the quotes cited may not have been written by Peter and may not reflect what Peter actually thought. Such is the nature of biblical scholarship.

109   Cf. New American Bible note regarding 2 Peter 3:16.

110   Paul's Pastoral Epistles to Timothy and Titus were not studied at this time. Nor was Hebrews, which was and/or is attributed to Paul by some.

111 *Our Sunday Visitor's Catholic Encyclopedia,* "Tradition" on page 971. Tradition includes: the major writings and teachings of the Fathers, the liturgical life of the Church, the living and lived faith of the whole Church down through the centuries, and the customs, institutions, and practices which express the Christian faith.

112 McKenzie, *Dictionary of the Bible*, 651.

113 Peter J. Kreeft, *Catholic Christianity*, (San Francisco: Ignatius Press, 2001), 25.

114 McKenzie, *Dictionary of the Bible*, 293.

115 McKenzie, *Dictionary of the Bible*, 651.

Chapter 8: Does God Care?

116 "Doctor of the Church" is a special title accorded by the Church to certain saints, whose theological teachings and writings are exceptional, in that they express both orthodoxy and a depth of understanding.

Appendix

117 *Encyclopedic Dictionary and Biblical Reference Guide* – located at the end of the Catholic Parish Edition of the *New American Bible* (Wichita, KS: Catholic Bible Publishers, 1994-1995 Edition).

118 The current edition of the New American Bible (that can be accessed online) was released on March 9, 2011. The prayers that are included in this book were inspired by the verses in a 1994-1995 edition of the NAB, as cited previously.

119 This column will be left blank for now. Its use will become apparent later.

120 Quote from the *Apostolic Constitution Fidei Depositum*, which was printed as an introduction to the *Catechism of the Catholic Church* (English translation for the United States of America). San Francisco: Ignatius Press, 1994, 5.

121 Peter J. Kreeft, *Catholic Christianity,* (Ignatius Press: San Francisco, 2001) Cf. 379-380.

122 380.

123 Cf. 381-382.

124 St. Augustine, as cited in CCC 2559.

Made in the USA
Monee, IL
30 March 2024

56129068R00101